Steck-Vaughn

TABE FUNDAMENTALS

Focus on Skills

LEVEL D Reading

Reviewers

Victor Gathers
Regional Coordinator of Adult Services
New York City Department of Education
Brooklyn Adult Learning Center
Brooklyn, New York

Brannon Lentz
Assistant Director of Adult Education/Skills
Training
Northwest Shoals Community College
Muscle Shoals, Alabama

Jean Pierre-Pipkin, Ed.D.
Director of Beaumont I.S.D. Adult Education
Cooperative Consortium
Beaumont, Texas

D1709795

STECK-VAUGHN
Harcourt Supplemental Publishers

www.steck-vaughn.com

Acknowledgments

Supervising Editor: Julie Higgins

Editor: Sharon Sargent

Associate Director of Design: Joyce Spicer

Supervising Designer: Pamela Heaney

Production Manager: Mychael Ferris

Production Coordinator: Heather Jernt

Senior Media Researcher: Alyx Kellington

Design and Composition: The Format Group, LLC

Photo Credits: P. iv ©Bluestone Productions/SuperStock Royalty Free; p. 2 ©HIRB/Index Stock Imagery; p. 4 ©Bob Daemmrich/The Image Works; p. 6 ©Spencer Grant/PhotoEdit; p. 49 ©Bettmann/CORBIS.

Illustrations: Pp. 26, 74, 78, 82 Francine Mastrangelo; pp. 45, 50, 55, 57, 66, 70, 84 Bob Novak.

From "Where the Red Fern Grows" by Wilson Rawls, copyright © 1961 by Sophie S. Rawls, Trustee, or successor Trustee(s) of the Rawls Trust, dated July 31, 1991. Copyright © 1961 by The Curtis Publishing Company. Used by permission of Random House Children's Books, a division of Random House, Inc. (p. 78)

ISBN 0-7398-8022-5

Printed in the United States of America.

1 2 3 4 5 6 7 8 9 0 TPO 09 08 07 06 05 04 03

Contents

To the Learner

Congratulations on your decision to study for the TABE! You are taking an important step in your educational career. This book will help you do your best on the TABE. You'll also find hints and strategies that will help you prepare for test day. Practice these skills—your success lies in your hands.

What Is the TABE?

TABE stands for the Tests of Adult Basic Education. These paper-and-pencil tests, published by McGraw-Hill, measure your progress on basic skills. There are five tests in all: Reading, Mathematics Computation, Applied Mathematics, Language, and Spelling.

TABE Levels M, D, and A

Test	Number of Items	Suggested Working Time (in minutes)
1 Reading	50	50
2 Mathematics Computation	25	15
3 Applied Mathematics	50	50
4 Language	55	39
5 Spelling	20	10

Test 1 Reading

This test measures basic reading skills. The main concepts covered by this test are word meaning, critical thinking, and understanding basic information.

Many things on this test will look familiar to you. They include documents and forms necessary to your everyday life, such as directions, bank statements, maps, and consumer labels. The test also includes items that measure your ability to find and use information from a dictionary, table of contents, or library computer display. The TABE also tests a learner's understanding of fiction and nonfiction passages.

Test 2 Mathematics Computation

Test 2 covers adding, subtracting, multiplying, and dividing. On the test you must use these skills with whole numbers, fractions, decimals, integers, and percents.

The skills covered in the Mathematics Computation test are the same skills you use daily to balance your checkbook, double a recipe, or fix your car.

Test 3 Applied Mathematics

The Applied Mathematics test links mathematical ideas to real-world situations. Many things you do every day require basic math. Making budgets, cooking, and doing your taxes all take math. The test covers pre-algebra, algebra, and geometry, too. Adults need to use all these skills.

Some questions will relate to one theme. Auto repairs could be the subject, for example. The question could focus on the repair schedule. For example, you know when you last had your car repaired. You also know how often you have to get it repaired. You might have to predict the next maintenance date.

Many of the items will not require you to use a specific strategy or formula to get the correct answer. Instead this test challenges you to use your own problem-solving strategies to answer the question.

Test 4 Language

The Language test asks you to analyze different types of writing. Examples are business letters, resumes, job reports, and essays. For each task, you have to show you understand good writing skills.

The questions fit adult interests and concerns. Some questions ask you to think about what is wrong in the written material. In other cases, you will correct sentences and paragraphs.

Test 5 Spelling

In everyday life, you need to spell correctly, especially in the workplace. The spelling words on this test are words that many people misspell and words that are commonly used in adult writing.

Test-Taking Tips

1. Read the directions very carefully. Make sure you read through them word for word. If you are not sure what the question says, ask the person giving the test to explain it to you.

2. Read each question carefully. Make sure you know what it means and what you have to do.

3. Read all of the answers carefully, even if you think you know the answer.

4. Make sure that the reading supports your answer. Don't answer without checking the reading. Don't rely only on outside knowledge.

5. Answer all of the questions. If you can't find the right answer, rule out the answers that you know are wrong. Then try to figure out the right answer. If you still don't know, make your best guess.

6. If you can't figure out the answer, put a light mark by the question and come back to it later. Erase your marks before you finish.

7. Don't change an answer unless you are sure your first answer is wrong. Usually your first idea is the correct answer.

8. If you get nervous, stop for a while. Take a few breaths and relax. Then start working again.

How to Use *TABE Fundamentals*

Step-by-Step Instruction In Levels M and D, each lesson starts with step-by-step instruction on a skill. The instruction contains examples and then a test example with feedback. This instruction is followed by practice questions. Work all of the questions in the lesson's practice and then check your work in the Answers and Explanations in the back of the book.

The Level A books contain practice for each skill covered on the TABE. Work all of the practice questions and then check your work in the Answers and Explanations in the back of the book.

Reviews The lessons in Levels M and D are grouped by a TABE Objective. At the end of each TABE Objective, there is a Review. Use these Reviews to find out if you need to review any of the lessons before continuing.

Performance Assessment At the end of every book, there is a special section called the Performance Assessment. This section is similar to the TABE test. It has the same number and type of questions. This assessment will give you an idea of what the real test is like.

Answer Sheet At the back of the book is a practice bubble-in answer sheet. Practice bubbling in your answers. Fill in the answer sheet carefully. For each answer, mark only one numbered space on the answer sheet. Mark the space beside the number that corresponds to the question. Mark only one answer per question. On the real TABE, if you have more than one answer per question, they will be scored as incorrect. Be sure to erase any stray marks.

Strategies and Hints Pay careful attention to the TABE Strategies and Hints throughout this book. Strategies are test-taking tips that help you do better on the test. Hints give you extra information about a skill.

Setting Goals

On the following page is a form to help you set your goals. Setting goals will help you get more from your work in this book.

Section 1. Why do you want to do well on the TABE? Take some time now to set your short-term and long-term goals on page 3.

Section 2. Making a schedule is one way to set priorities. Deadlines will help you stay focused on the steps you need to take to reach your goals.

Section 3. Your goals may change over time. This is natural. After a month, for example, check the progress you've made. Do you need to add new goals or make any changes to the ones you have? Checking your progress on a regular basis helps you reach your goals.

> For more information on setting goals, see Steck-Vaughn's *Start Smart Goal Setting Strategies*.

1. Set Your Goals

What is your long-term goal for using this book?

_____
_____
_____
_____

Complete these areas to identify the smaller steps to take to reach your long-term goal.

Content area	What I Know	What I Want to Learn
Reading	_____	_____
Language	_____	_____
Spelling	_____	_____
Math	_____	_____
Other	_____	_____

2. Make a Schedule

Set some deadlines for yourself.

For a 20-week planning calendar, see Steck-Vaughn's *Start Smart Planner.*

Goals	Begin Date	End Date
_____	_____	_____
_____	_____	_____
_____	_____	_____
_____	_____	_____
_____	_____	_____

3. Celebrate Your Success

Note the progress you've made. If you made changes in your goals, record them here.

_____
_____
_____
_____
_____

To the Instructor

About TABE 7 and 8

The Tests of Adult Basic Education are designed to meet the needs of adult learners in ABE programs. Written and designed to be relevant to adult learners' lives and interests, this material focuses on the life, job, academic, and problem-solving skills that the typical adult needs.

Because of the increasing importance of thinking skills in any curriculum, *TABE Fundamentals* focuses on critical thinking throughout each TABE Objective.

The TABE identifies the following thinking processes as essential to learning and achieving goals in daily life:

◆ Gather Information   ◆ Generate Ideas
◆ Organize Information   ◆ Synthesize Elements
◆ Analyze Information   ◆ Evaluate Outcomes

Test 1 Reading

The TABE measures an adult's ability to understand home, workplace, and academic texts. The ability to construct meaning from prose and visual information is also covered through reading and analyzing diagrams, maps, charts, forms, and consumer materials.

Test 2 Mathematics Computation

This test covers whole numbers, decimals, fractions, integers, percents, and algebraic expressions. Skills are carefully targeted to the appropriate level of difficulty.

Test 3 Applied Mathematics

This test emphasizes problem-solving and critical-thinking skills, with a focus on the life-skill applications of mathematics. Estimation and pattern-recognition skills also are important on this test.

Test 4 Language

The Language test focuses on writing and effective communication. Students examine writing samples that need revision, with complete-sentence and paragraph contexts for the various items. The tests emphasize editing, proofreading, and other key skills. The context of the questions are real-life settings appropriate to adults.

Test 5 Spelling

This test focuses on the words learners most typically misspell. In this way, the test identifies the spelling skills learners most need in order to communicate effectively. Items typically present high-frequency words in short sentences.

Uses of the TABE

There are three basic uses of the TABE:

Instructional

From an instructional point of view, the TABE allows instructors to assess students' entry levels as they begin an adult program. The TABE also allows instructors to diagnose learners' strengths and weaknesses in order to determine appropriate areas to focus instruction. Finally the TABE allows instructors and institutions to monitor learners' progress.

Administrative

The TABE allows institutions to assess classes in general and measure the effectiveness of instruction and whether learners are making progress.

Governmental

The TABE provides a means of assessing a school's or program's effectiveness.

The National Reporting System (NRS) and the TABE

Adult education and literacy programs are federally funded and thus accountable to the federal government. The National Reporting System monitors adult education. Developed with the help of adult educators, the NRS sets the reporting requirements for adult education programs around the country. The information collected by the NRS is used to assess the effectiveness of adult education programs and make necessary improvements.

A key measure defined by the NRS is educational gain, which is an assessment of the improvement in learners' reading, writing, speaking, listening, and other skills during their instruction. Programs assess educational gain at every stage of instruction.

NRS Functioning Levels	Grade Levels	TABE (7–8) scaled scores
Beginning ABE Literacy	0–1.9	Reading . . . . 367 and below Total Math . . . . 313 and below Language . . . . . 391 and below
Beginning Basic Education	2–3.9	Reading . . . . 368–460 Total Math . . . . 393–490 Language 393–490
Low Intermediate Basic Education	4–5.9	Reading . . . . 461–517 Total Math . . . . 442–505 Language 491–523
High Intermediate Basic Education	6–8.9	Reading . . . . 518–566 Total Math . . . . 506–565 Language 524–559
Low Adult Secondary Education	9–10.9	Reading . . . . 567–595 Total Math . . . . 566–594 Language 560–585

According to the NRS guidelines, states select the method of assessment appropriate for their needs. States can assess educational gain either through standardized tests or through performance-based assessment. Among the standardized tests typically used under NRS guidelines is the TABE, which meets the NRS standards both for administrative procedures and for scoring.

The three main methods used by the NRS to collect data are the following:

1. **Direct program reporting,** from the moment of student enrollment
2. **Local follow-up surveys,** involving learners' employment or academic goals
3. **Data matching,** or sharing data among agencies serving the same clients so that outcomes unique to each program can be identified.

Two of the major goals of the NRS are academic achievement and workplace readiness. Educational gain is a means to reaching these goals. As learners progress through the adult education curriculum, the progress they make should help them either obtain or keep employment or obtain a diploma, whether at the secondary school level or higher. The TABE is flexible enough to meet both the academic and workplace goals set forth by the NRS.

Using *TABE Fundamentals*

Adult Basic Education Placement

From the outset, the TABE allows effective placement of learners. You can use the *TABE Fundamentals* series to support instruction of those skills where help is needed.

High School Equivalency

Placement often involves predicting learners' success on the GED, the high school equivalency exam. Each level of *TABE Fundamentals* covers Reading, Language, Spelling, Applied and Computational Math to allow learners to focus their attention where it is needed.

Assessing Progress

Each TABE skill is covered in a lesson. These lessons are grouped by TABE Objective. At the end of each TABE Objective, there is a Review. Use these Reviews to find out if the learners need to review any of the skills before continuing.

At the end of the book, there is a special section called the Performance Assessment. This section is similar to the TABE test. It has the same number and type of questions. You can use the Performance Assessment as a timed pretest or posttest with your learners, or as a more general review for the actual TABE.

Steck-Vaughn's *TABE Fundamentals* Program at a Glance

The charts on the following page provide a quick overview of the elements of Steck-Vaughn's *TABE Fundamentals* series. Use this chart to match the TABE objectives with the skill areas for each level. This chart will come in handy whenever you need to find which objectives fit the specific skill areas you need to cover.

Steck-Vaughn's *TABE Fundamentals* Program at a Glance

TABE OBJECTIVE	Level M		Level D		Level A
	Reading	Language and Spelling	Reading	Language and Spelling	Reading, Language, and Spelling
Reading					
Interpret Graphic Information	◆		◆		◆
Words in Context	◆		◆		◆
Recall Information	◆		◆		◆
Construct Meaning	◆		◆		◆
Evaluate/Extend Meaning	◆		◆		◆
Language					
Usage		◆		◆	◆
Sentence Formation		◆		◆	◆
Paragraph Development		◆		◆	◆
Punctuation and Capitalization		◆		◆	◆
Writing Convention		◆		◆	◆
Spelling					
Vowel		◆		◆	◆
Consonant		◆		◆	◆
Structural Unit		◆		◆	◆

TABE OBJECTIVE	Level M		Level D		Level A
	Math Computation	Applied Math	Math Computation	Applied Math	Computational and Applied Math
Mathematics Computation					
Addition of Whole Numbers	◆				
Subtraction of Whole Numbers	◆				
Multiplication of Whole Numbers	◆		◆		
Division of Whole Numbers	◆		◆		
Decimals	◆		◆		◆
Fractions	◆		◆		◆
Integers			◆		◆
Percents			◆		◆
Algebraic Operations					◆
Applied Mathematics					
Numeration		◆		◆	
Number Theory		◆		◆	
Data Interpretation		◆		◆	
Pre-Algebra and Algebra		◆		◆	
Measurement		◆		◆	
Geometry		◆		◆	
Computation in Context		◆		◆	
Estimation		◆		◆	

Lesson 1 Dictionary Usage

Dictionaries can be used to find the meanings of words. They contain definitions. A definition is a description of a word's meaning. On the TABE you will have to choose the definition that best fits with the meaning of a word used in a passage.

Example **Read this paragraph. Use the dictionary entry to determine the meaning of the word *follow* in the paragraph. Circle the number of the correct definition.**

The soldier had trained nearly a year to fight in the war. He was prepared to follow the captain's orders and go into battle.

This is the correct phonetic pronunciation of the word.

The part of speech term tells if the word is a noun, verb, adjective, or some other part of speech.

Dictionary entries show how a word can be divided.

fol·low (fäl'ō) *Verb.* 1. To go behind or come after. 2. To keep up with and understand: *Try to follow the major's speech.* 3. To imitate or copy. 4. To obey or act according to. 5. To take as one's work: *She hopes to follow a career in law.*

Definitions often include an example sentence that includes the defined word. All of the numbered definitions provide different meanings for the word.

Did you circle definition 4? In this paragraph *follow* means "to obey or act according to." This is correct because the soldier was ready to obey or act according to his captain's orders.

Test Example

Read the paragraph. Then answer the question by circling the letter of the best answer.

It is important to keep your dog secure when you take it for a walk. One way you can prevent your dog from running away is to use a leash. A leash will allow the dog to follow you closely as you walk.

1 Which definition of the word *follow* is used in the paragraph?

A Definition 1

B Definition 2

C Definition 3

D Definition 4

TABE Strategy

Try substituting each definition in place of the word in the sentence. Then read the sentence using the substitution. If the meaning of the sentence stays the same, it should be a match.

1 A The word *follow* in this paragraph means "to go behind or come after." The dog cannot *understand* you closely (option B) or *copy* you closely (option C). Although a dog can *obey* (follow orders), a dog cannot *obey* or *act according to* you closely (option D).

Read the paragraph. Then read the statement and the dictionary entry for each question. Circle the letter of the best answer.

Ever since I got my first job, I have made it a principle to save money each month. My first job was not a big moneymaker. Every sunny day for one entire summer, I would carry a pitcher of ice-cold lemonade to sell by the roadside. It was that summer that I built up my resistance to spending available cash. After all, the candy store was just three blocks away. The reward finally came when I used my savings to purchase my first ten-speed bicycle. Then I proudly peddled past all the neighborhood kids on their daily walk to the candy store.

The paragraph says, "Ever since I got my first job, I have made it a *principle* to save money each month." Here is part of a dictionary entry for the word *principle*. Use it to answer number 1.

prin·ci·ple (prin′səpəl) *Noun.* 1. A basic truth or law. 2. A rule of action or conduct. 3. A rule of science explaining how things act. 4. Goodness; honesty: *a person of principle.* 5. A basic belief: *religious principles.*

 Which definition of the word *principle* is used in the paragraph?

A Definition 2

B Definition 3

C Definition 4

D Definition 5

The paragraph says, "Every sunny day for one entire summer, I would *carry* a pitcher of ice-cold lemonade to sell by the roadside." Here is part of a dictionary entry for the word *carry*. Use it to answer number 2.

carry (kar′ē) *Verb.* 1. To continue or extend. 2. To hold onto something and take it somewhere. 3. To sing: *to carry a tune.* 4. To transfer a number from one place or column in the sum to the next. 5. To offer something for sale: *The store carries my favorite brand of jeans.*

 Which definition of the word *carry* is used in the paragraph?

F Definition 1

G Definition 2

H Definition 3

J Definition 4

The paragraph says, "It was that summer that I built up my *resistance* to spending available cash." Here is part of a dictionary entry for the word *resistance*. Use it to answer number 3.

re·sist·ance (ri zis′təns) *Noun.* 1. People who secretly organize and fight for freedom from a controlling power. 2. A force that opposes the motion of an object. 3. A property of a conductor that opposes the passage of an electric current and changes electric energy into heat. 4. The ability to fight off or overcome: *He developed a sore throat because his resistance was low.*

 Which definition of the word *resistance* is used in the paragraph?

A Definition 1

B Definition 2

C Definition 3

D Definition 4

Check your answers on page 86.

Lesson 2 | Index

An index is located at the end of most books. It contains an alphabetized list of the book's contents and the page numbers where specific information can be found. If you know how to use an index, you will be able to locate information in a book quickly and efficiently.

Example **Look at this section of an index page from a car service manual. Suppose your car's clutch is loose and you want to fix it. On what page would you find information on how to adjust the clutch? Circle the page number.**

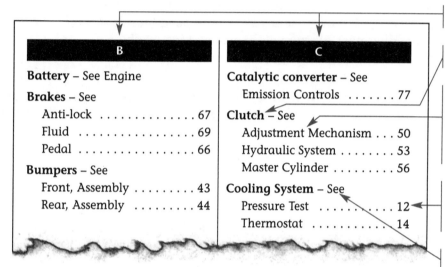

B	
Battery – See Engine	
Brakes – See	
Anti-lock 67	
Fluid 69	
Pedal 66	
Bumpers – See	
Front, Assembly 43	
Rear, Assembly 44	

C	
Catalytic converter – See	
Emission Controls 77	
Clutch – See	
Adjustment Mechanism . . . 50	
Hydraulic System 53	
Master Cylinder 56	
Cooling System – See	
Pressure Test 12	
Thermostat 14	

Entries in an index are arranged in alphabetical order.

Index listings are topics or sub-topics.

Sometimes an index topic has a lot of information about it so it will be broken down into sub-topics. Sub-topics are listed under the topic to which they belong. Sub-topics are listed in alphabetical order.

The page number where the information can be found is directly to the right of each topic or sub-topic.

The word *See* directs you from a topic to another topic or subtopic.

Information on clutch adjustments is on page 50. The number 50 is to the right of the sub-topic "adjustment mechanism" under the topic "Clutch."

Test Example

Refer to the car service manual index above. Then do number 1. Circle the letter of the correct answer.

1   If you want to read about how to repair your anti-lock brakes, on which page would you look for that information?

   A   69

   B   66

   C   33

   D   67

Hint

When trying to locate specific information in an index, think of possible general topics under which it might be listed. Specific information is often listed as a sub-topic of a general topic.

1   **D**   Page 67 has information about anti-lock brakes. Option A is not correct because page 69 has information about brake fluid. Option B is not correct because page 66 has information about the brake pedal. Page 33 is not in this portion of the index (option C).

Study this index page from a home improvement book. Then answer numbers 1 through 4 by circling the letter of the best answer.

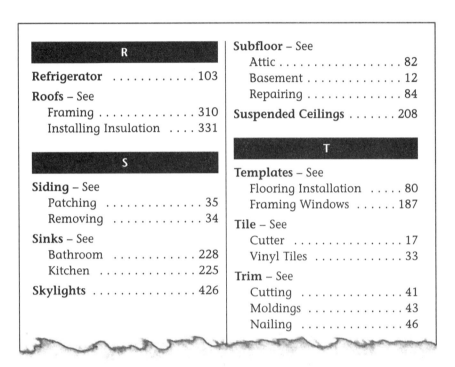

1 If you want to repair a small hole on the vinyl siding of a house, on which page will you look?

A 84

B 35

C 34

D 33

2 Which of these <u>cannot</u> be found on this index page?

F Trim

G Templates

H Tile

J Two-slot receptacle

3 Which of these is listed on Page 208?

A vinyl tiles

B framing windows

C suspended ceilings

D flooring installation

4 Suppose you want to install a new drain in the bathroom sink. On which page will you find information on how to do this?

F 228

G 225

H 331

J 84

Check your answers on page 86.

Lesson 3 Reference Sources

Reference sources are used to find information. Being familiar with all kinds of reference sources will help you decide which is most useful when you need to look up something. On the TABE you will have to decide which reference source has the information being asked for in the question. You will also be asked how to give credit to a reference that is written into a report.

Example If you were looking for a famous saying from Dr. Martin Luther King Jr.,

which would be the best reference source to use? _____

Look at the chart below to review the different types and purposes of common reference sources.

Reference Source	What It Is	Why It Is Used
almanac	a calendar-like book that gives facts and statistics about government, economics, sports, and other topics	to quickly locate facts and figures about topics
anthology	a collection of writing	to read a collection of the same kind of writing, such as short stories or poems
atlas	a book of maps, sometimes with historical and statistical information	to get geographic information or to locate a place
book of quotations	a book that has sayings from famous people	to quickly find a quote
encyclopedia	a book that has articles on subjects, arranged in alphabetical order	to get brief explanations of things in our world
magazine	a publication that has articles about different topics of interest	to read for pleasure or to find out about topics in the news

Famous sayings from Martin Luther King, Jr. would be in a book of quotations.

Example If you wanted to use a quote from a book for a report you are writing,

how would you give the author credit? _____

_____

Any time you quote any author you should give credit. **To give credit, note the book source in a footnote at the bottom of the page.** A footnote has information about the book such as the title, author, and the page number on which the quote was found.

Test Example

Read the question. Circle the letter of the best answer.

1 When writing a paper, if you use the exact words of an author you should

   A put a line under the quote in your paper

   B copy the quote in the bibliography

   C footnote the source of the quote

   D write the author's name on the title page of your paper

1 C Option C is the correct answer. Just putting a line under a quote (option A) would not show where it came from. Copying the quote (option B) would also not tell where the quote came from. Option D is not correct because the quote source does not belong on a title page.

Practice

Answer numbers 1 through 6 by circling the letter of the best answer.

1 You would probably find the most sayings by Thomas Jefferson in

A an atlas

B an encyclopedia

C a book of quotations

D an anthology of short stories

2 The fastest way to find out where Charlottesville is in the state of Virginia would be to look in

F an atlas

G an almanac

H a magazine

J a book of quotations

3 If you directly quote the author of a book in a report you are writing about Thomas Jefferson, you should

A highlight the quotation

B use a footnote to credit the source

C write the author's name at the top of the report

D include all the books written by the author in the bibliography

4 Which of these would probably be the best source of information about the inventions of Thomas Jefferson?

F *Architectural Design*

G *The Writer's Notebook*

H *Thomas Jefferson's Inventions*

J *The History of the Copy Machine*

5 If you wanted a brief explanation of Jefferson's major contributions, in which of these reference sources would you look?

A an atlas

B an encyclopedia

C a book of quotations

D an anthology of short stories

6 Jefferson designed his own hilltop house in Charlottesville, Virginia. If you were interested in buying land and building a house in Charlottesville, which of these reference sources would you use?

F an atlas

G an encyclopedia

H *Charlottesville Real Estate Weekly*

J *The History of Virginia*

Check your answers on page 86.

Lesson 4 Forms

A form is a document with blank spaces for writing information. Different forms have different purposes. Some common types of forms include tax forms and job applications. The TABE will ask questions about using information from a paragraph to correctly fill out a form.

Example **Read the paragraph and study the job application form below. What should Maria write under the "Employment Experience" part of the form? _____**

Maria Santos needs a job. She recently saw a help-wanted ad in the window of a local childcare center. Maria thought the job would be perfect for her, so she asked about the position and got an application. Maria loves taking care of kids. For the past six months, Maria has earned money looking after her neighbor's baby.

The "Personal and Background Information" section is where Maria will write basic information about herself, such as her name and address.

The "Education" section is where Maria will write about the schools she has attended.

The "Employment Experience" section is where Maria will list the jobs that she has had.

The "Special Skills and Qualifications" section is where Maria will list her childcare skills.

APPLICATION FOR EMPLOYMENT

Directions: Fill out all of the information in the spaces provided below. If you are called for an interview, please bring 3 letters of reference from past employers.

PERSONAL AND BACKGROUND INFORMATION

Name (first, last) _____

Address _____

_____

_____

Home phone _____ Work phone _____

EDUCATION

High School _____

Number of years completed _____

Trade School/College/Further Education _____

Number of years completed _____

Degree/Certificate _____

EMPLOYMENT EXPERIENCE

Directions: Start with your present or most recent job. Include babysitting, summer camp, teaching, day care, and volunteer work experience.

Employer _____

Length of employment _____

Your position _____

Employer _____

Length of employment _____

Your position _____

SPECIAL SKILLS AND QUALIFICATIONS

Directions: Summarize special skills and qualifications that relate to working with children.

_____

_____

_____

---

14 • TABE Fundamentals

Reading

Maria's husband Tom wrote her a list of directions for filling out the form for her to take with her.

> Good Luck! And remember to:
> – Read the entire application before you fill it out.
> – Read the directions at the top of the form. They apply to the entire form.
> – Look at how the form is broken into sections.
> – Read the section headings to understand each section's purpose.
> – When you have read the form, think about what you need to write on it.

What should Maria write under the "Employment Experience" part of the form? Maria should include her babysitting job under the "Employment Experience" part of the form. The directions in this section tell Maria to include babysitting, summer camp, teaching, day care, and volunteer work experience. Taking care of her neighbor's baby was babysitting work.

Test Example

Read the paragraph below. Use the information from the paragraph and the form on page 14 to answer the question.

Maria also volunteers every Saturday at a nearby women's shelter. She plays with the toddlers and holds the babies. At the women's shelter, Maria was given training in first aid and CPR. She hopes this training will help her get the new job.

1 Under which part of the form should Maria write about her training in first aid and CPR?

A Education

B References

C Special Skills and Qualifications

D Personal and Background Information

---

1 C Having first-aid and CPR training are skills that are considered valuable in working with children. They involve emergency care-giving. Maria should include this information in the "Special Skills and Qualifications" section of the form. Options A, B, and D are not correct because those sections ask for different information about Maria.

Practice

Study the employee information form. Then read the paragraph. Answer the questions by circling the letter of the best answer.

EMPLOYEE INFORMATION

Directions: Read and fill out the form completely. This information is for your safety. It may be used in case of an emergency. This information will be kept private.

PERSONAL INFORMATION

Name _____

Address _____

_____

_____

Home phone _____ Work phone _____

Date of birth _____

Social Security Number _____

Health care provider _____

Insurance policy number _____

MEDICAL INFORMATION

Please list all medications that you are currently taking _____

_____

_____

Please list any allergies to food or medicine that you have _____

_____

_____

Please list past injuries and illnesses and other important medical information _____

_____

_____

_____

EMERGENCY CONTACT INFORMATION

Name of person to contact in case of emergency _____

_____

Address _____

_____

Telephone numbers where your emergency contact can be reached

Home _____ Work _____

Maria got a job as a day-care provider. Her responsibilities include looking after a group of toddlers every morning. She will be starting her job in one week. Her new employer has asked her to fill out an employee information form. Maria was told that the form may be used if there is an emergency. Her husband, Tom, will help her fill out the form. He reminds Maria to write that she is allergic to bee stings.

1 This form is used to gather information about

A a boss

B a child

C a spouse

D an employee

2 Which of these should <u>not</u> be included in the "Personal Information" section?

F Maria's name

G Maria's phone number

H Maria's allergy to bee stings

J Maria's health provider card number

3 On what part of the form should Maria write her husband's name and work phone number?

A Directions

B Medical Information

C Personal Information

D Emergency Contact Information

4 Who could someday be shown the information that Maria wrote on the form?

F a doctor

G another employee

H a child at the day care center

J a parent of a child who attends the day care center

5 Which of these should be written in the "Medical Information" section?

A Maria's allergy to bee stings

B Maria's social security number

C Maria's CPR certification number

D Maria's home and work phone numbers

Check your answers on pages 86–87.

Library Catalog Display

Libraries keep records of all their books and materials. The records show information about each item such as the title, author, and date published. Many libraries have this information stored in a computer database. When you do a computer search for library materials, you can type in a subject and view the screen display of matches.

Example Anthony wants to listen to the blues. He has a cassette player. He goes to the library and uses the computer to find out what is available. Which choice on the display is the best choice for Anthony's needs? Circle the number of the best choice.

YOUR SUBJECT: BLUES MUSIC	DATE	FORMAT
1. The Blues of the Early Years	1967	Record
2. Collection from the Blues Masters	1989	Cassette
3. The History of Blues Music	1984	CD
4. How to Play the Blues Guitar	2001	Video
5. Jazz and Blues from the Blue Ridge Mountains	1990	DVD
6. The Great Legends of Blues Music	2000	Book

Anthony sees that there are 6 numbered results. To figure out which item best meets his needs, he first reads the headings: *Subject, Date,* and *Format.*

- The **Subject** column shows the titles of the items.
- The **Date** column shows the year each item was published.
- The **Format** column tells how each title is published, as a book, cassette, video, CD, DVD, or record.

Number 2 is the best choice. Because Anthony wants to listen to a cassette, he knows that there is only one result that meets his needs. *Collection from the Blues Masters* is a cassette tape with music from famous blues musicians.

Test Example

Anthony is interested in the blues. He is using the library computer to find out what is available. Study the computer display screen. Answer the question by circling the letter of the best answer.

1   How many different video selections does the computer display show?

A   one   C   three

B   two   D   six

1 **A** *How to Play the Blues Guitar* is the only video listed. Options B, C, and D are not correct because there is only one video on the display.

Practice

Madge is interested in churches. She is using the library computer to find out what materials are available. Study the computer display. Answer the questions by circling the letter of the best answer.

```
YOUR SUBJECT: CHURCH                       DATE     FORMAT
 1. Classical Church Music                 1965     Record
 2. Constructing a Modern Church           1999     Video
 3. Great Churches of the 17th Century     1989     Book
 4. Gospel Music Selections               2000     Cassette
 5. The History of Notre Dame             1954     Book
 6. Gothic Churches                       1998     Book
 7. Chanting and Meditations              2001     Cassette
 8. Photographs of Stained Glass          1992     Book
 9. A Tour of France's Cathedrals         1987     Video
10. Great Churches of the Americas        2000     DVD
```

1 How many different written selections does the computer display show?

A two

B three

C four

D nine

2 Which of these should Madge choose if she wants to watch a church being built?

F *Gothic Churches*

G *Photographs of Stained Glass*

H *A Tour of France's Cathedrals*

J *Constructing a Modern Church*

3 Which of these should Madge choose if she is interested in reading about different churches built in the Gothic style?

A *Great Churches of the 17th Century*

B *The History of Notre Dame*

C *Photographs of Stained Glass*

D *Gothic Churches*

4 Which of these should Madge choose if she wants to listen to music on her record player?

F *Classical Church Music*

G *Gospel Music Selections*

H *Chanting and Meditations*

J *A Tour of France's Cathedrals*

Check your answers on page 87.

Lesson 6 Maps

People use maps to navigate around towns, cities, states, and countries. Knowing how to read a map is a skill that makes traveling much easier. Being able to determine the shortest route to a place will save you time. Being able to understand map symbols and directions will help you travel to a new place without getting lost.

Example **Look at the road map below. In what direction would you travel to go from Rocky Mountain National Park to Mesa Verde National Park?_____**

_____

Highway Map of Colorado

Look at the compass rose at the top left part of the map. Each letter stands for the 4 major directions: north, east, south, and west. The arrows in between are a combination of the major directions on either side. For example, *southeast* is in between *south* and *east*.

Locate Rocky Mountain National Park and Mesa Verde National Park on the map. Draw a straight line from Rocky Mountain National Park to Mesa Verde National Park. Look at the compass rose and use it to determine what direction the line is pointing. **You would travel southwest.**

Test Example

Answer the question by circling the letter of the best answer.

1   What is the most direct route from Pueblo, Colorado to the state of Wyoming?

   A   west on Interstate 70

   B   north on Interstate 25

   C   Interstate 25 to Interstate 70

   D   Interstate 25 to Interstate 76

Hint

The words *from* and *to* are key words in the question. The word *from* indicates that you start at Pueblo, Colorado. The word *to* indicates that you end in Wyoming.

1 **B** Interstate 25 crosses through Colorado and Wyoming. It goes right through Pueblo and continues north into Wyoming. Options A and C are not correct because from Colorado, Interstate 70 goes east into Kansas or west into Utah. Option D is not correct because from Pueblo, Interstate 76 heads northeast into Nebraska.

Practice

Study the highway map below. Answer the questions by circling the letter of the best answer.

Map of Southwick, MA and Surrounding Area

1 In what direction would you need to travel to go from Hosmer Corner to Vining Hill?

A northeast

B southeast

C southwest

D northwest

2 Which place is furthest east on the map?

F Vining Hill

G Gillett Corner

H Hosmer Corner

J Southwick

3 Which is the most direct route from Congamond Lakes to Hosmer Corner?

A 168 to 202 to 57

B 168 to 57 to 202

C 57 to 202 to 168

D 202 to 168 to 57

Check your answers on page 87.

Amy is using the library computer to find out what materials are available about Elvis Presley. Study the computer display. Then answer number 1.

YOUR SUBJECT: ELVIS PRESLEY	DATE	FORMAT
1. The Biography of Elvis Presley	1980	Book
2. Elvis: The Early Years	1978	Cassette
3. The King of Rock-and-Roll	1988	Book
4. Last Train to Memphis	1994	Book

1 Which of these should Amy choose if she wants to hear some of Elvis Presley's music?

   A *Last Train to Memphis*

   B *Elvis: The Early Years*

   C *The King of Rock-and-Roll*

   D *The Biography of Elvis Presley*

2 The fastest way to find the location of a small town in Tennessee would be to look in

   F an atlas

   G an almanac

   H a travel magazine

   J an anthology of poetry

Look at the map below. Then answer number 3.

Highway Map of Southwest Tennessee

3 Amy is planning a trip to Graceland, Elvis's home in Memphis. Which is the most direct route from her home in Jackson to southwest Tennessee?

   A Highway 45

   B Interstate 40

   C Interstate 55

   D Highway 79

Study this part of an index page from a book about Elvis Presley. Then answer number 4.

S
Smith, Junior –
Elvis's army service 29
recording sessions 76
Stoker, Gordon –
Elvis's talent 34
recordings with Elvis 33
Sullivan, Ed –
TV appearances with 99

4   If Amy wants to find out more about Elvis's recording sessions with Junior Smith, on which page would she look?

F 29

G 33

H 76

J 99

Study this tour evaluation form. Then read the paragraph and the dictionary entry for the word *hold*. Answer numbers 5 and 6 by circling the letter of the best answer.

Graceland Tours Evaluation Form

Name _____ Date _____

Address _____

Phone number _____ E-mail address _____

Your tour guide's name _____

Comments/Feedback _____

At Graceland, Amy really likes the trophy building, but she wishes the tour had included a visit to the meditation garden. Amy's favorite part of the tour is Elvis's gravesite. When she sees his tombstone, she has to hold back her tears.

hold (hōld) *Verb*. 1. To keep in the hands; grasp. 2. To restrain or control; keep back. 3. To regard or consider. 4. To guard or occupy: *hold the fort*.

5   Which of these could Amy write on the form next to "Comments/Feedback"?

A I would have liked to have seen the trophy building.

B Amy Chan

C I would have liked to have seen the meditation garden.

D My favorite part of the tour was the meditation garden.

6   Which definition of the word *hold* is used in the paragraph?

F Definition 1

G Definition 2

H Definition 3

J Definition 4

Check your answers on page 87.

Lesson 7 · Same Meaning

When you read, you sometimes come across words you don't understand. When this happens, there are ways to figure out what a word means without using a dictionary. You can do this by reading the other words and sentences around the word very carefully. Doing this will give you clues about the meaning of the word. If you study a passage until you understand the overall meaning, you can often figure out the specific meaning of a difficult word.

Example **Tracy has been writing about her dreams in a journal. Read this section of her journal. What does the word *pursued* mean? _____**

> I woke up this morning with my heart pounding. I dreamed that I was being pursued by a black bear.

Did you write that *pursued* means being chased or followed? By reading the first sentence, you can conclude that the action in Tracy's dream made her feel scared. A black bear chasing a scared person would make the person's heart race and face sweat. If you substituted either *chased* or *followed* for the word *pursued*, the sentence would still fit with the meaning of the passage: I dreamed that I was being *chased* by a black bear.

Example **Read this sentence. It also uses the word *pursued*. What does *pursued* mean in this sentence? _____**

> George pursued a degree in nursing.

Did you write *worked towards*? In some test questions, there may be more than one correct meaning in the answer choices. In order to choose the *best* answer, carefully read *how* the word is used in the passage. For example, if this meaning of the word *pursued* is substituted in the sentence from the first example, it would not make sense: I dreamed that I was being *worked towards* by a black bear.

Test Example

Read the following excerpt from Tracy's journal. Answer the question by circling the letter of the best answer.

> In my dream I was running through the woods. Tree branches brushed my face as I ran. The black bear was getting closer and closer. I could feel my knees start to buckle. Just as I was about to fall, I woke up.

TABE Strategy

Read every answer. Substitute each answer for the word in the sentence and choose the answer that best fits with the meaning of the sentence and the passage.

1   What does the word *buckle* mean in the paragraph?

   A   to panic   C   a clasp on a belt

   B   to rub together   D   to bend or give way

1 **D** The word *buckle* in this paragraph means "to bend or give way." When you are about to fall, your knees give way. "To panic" means to suddenly show fear (option A). Knees cannot show fear. Buckle does not mean "to rub together" (option B). Although buckle does mean "a clasp on a belt," that definition does not fit the meaning of the sentence (option C).

Practice

Tracy keeps a journal of her dreams by her bedside. Read this entry. Answer the questions by circling the letter of the best answer.

I remember the sound of the cool wind *whipping* by my face. Two wings, *adorned* with soft, brown feathers, stretched far to the sides of my proud, majestic body. I *scanned* the ground below, looking for any signs of movement. The urgency of my search kept me focused and *determined*. I was an eagle, caught between the freedom of floating *effortlessly* through the cold night air and the *tingle* of hunger slowly moving through the whole of my body.

1 The author says that she remembers "the sound of the cool wind *whipping* by my face." In this context, the word *whipping* means the same as

A beating

B mixing

C blowing

D singing

2 The author describes the eagle's wings as *adorned* with soft, brown feathers. Which of these means the same as the word *adorned*?

F adhered

G admired

H traveled

J decorated

3 According to the paragraph, the eagle "*scanned* the ground below, looking for any signs of movement." What does the word *scanned* mean here?

A copied

B searched

C swindled

D traversed

4 The author says "the urgency of my search kept me focused and *determined*." What does the word *determined* mean in this sentence?

F awake

G steadfast

H defeated

J delighted

5 In the paragraph, the eagle is described as "floating *effortlessly*." In this context, the word *effortlessly* means the same as

A without pain

B without warmth

C without warning

D without force

6 The last sentence mentions the "*tingle* of hunger." What does the word *tingle* mean?

F a cold sensation

G a sudden movement

H a prickling sensation

J a feeling of alertness

Check your answers on pages 87–88.

Read this passage. Answer the questions by circling the letter of the best answer.

Sunday Supper

Sundays throughout my childhood were spent at my grandparents' house where supper was served at exactly two o'clock. My memory of the aroma of slow-baked, spice-covered chicken makes my stomach growl even now. In the distance, I could hear the sound of my mother and my grandmother talking, muffled only by a closed kitchen door. Their low voices seemed to blend together.

When the feast emerged from the kitchen, we were all called to the table. My brother and I sat at the far end, where we would indulge ourselves in the glory of our drumsticks. The conversation between the adults seemed to drag on in slow motion. I often slithered halfway off my chair to see the view from under the table. From there, I could see the thick folds of my grandmother's legs. Her dark stockings fell just under her knees. They stopped at a certain place that made me feel unsettled. I held back the desire to reach over and pull them up.

Dessert was cake and fruit eaten around the living room coffee table. My favorite fruit was, and still is, ripe pomegranate. I don't know what I liked better, opening the fruit or eating it. Watching my grandfather open a pomegranate was like watching a sculptor carving his way around a block of wood, slowly revealing the artwork that lay hidden beneath its layers. His teeth would pierce the skin, and I remember seeing little red spurts of sweet juice squirt from the edges of his mouth. Then he would place his thumbs under the exposed opening. He took a deep breath, clenched his teeth, and ripped the pomegranate apart. For that one moment in time, he was the toughest man in the world. My brother and I mimicked my grandfather, tearing our sections into smaller pieces with great force and strength.

1 According to the passage, the author remembers "the *aroma* of slow-baked, spice-covered chicken." What does the word *aroma* mean here?

  A taste

  B scent

  C sight

  D flavor

2 In the passage, the author recalls "My brother and I sat at the far end, where we would *indulge* ourselves in the glory of our drumsticks." What does the word *indulge* mean here?

  F to eat

  G to cover

  H to gratify

  J to embrace

3 According to the passage, "the feast *emerged* from the kitchen." What does the word *emerged* mean here?

  A spilled

  B was eaten

  C was cooked

  D came out of

4 The passage says that the conversation "seemed to *drag* on in slow motion." What does the word *drag* mean here?

  F pull

  G search

  H move slowly

  J move quickly

5 The passage says "Watching my grandfather open a pomegranate was like watching a sculptor carving his way around a block of wood, slowly revealing the artwork that lay hidden *beneath* its layers." What does the word *beneath* mean here?

  A above

  B beside

  C around

  D underneath

6 The author says his grandfather "was like a *sculptor* carving his way around a block of wood." What does the word *sculptor* mean here?

  F an artist

  G a builder

  H a butcher

  J an engineer

7 The author mentions the feeling of being *unsettled* by the sight of his grandmother's stockings. What does the word *unsettled* mean here?

  A uneasy

  B uneven

  C not paid

  D not focused

8 The last sentence says, "My brother and I *mimicked* my grandfather." What does the word *mimicked* mean here?

  F amused

  G imitated

  H irritated

  J introduced

Check your answers on page 88.

Lesson 8 ▸ Details

It is important to pay close attention to details when reading TABE passages. Details are the facts or the specific information that makes up a story. They tell *who, what, why, where, when,* and *how.* Noticing details helps you understand what you are reading.

Example **Read the paragraph below. Three of the details are underlined.**

> <u>Native Americans</u> lived peacefully in <u>North America</u> for hundreds of years. They first came in contact with European settlers in the <u>early 1600s</u>. While the Europeans had more sophisticated weapons technology, the Native Americans used <u>bows and arrows</u>.

This paragraph gives details that answer these questions: *Who? Where? When?* and *What?*

Find the detail in the paragraph that answers the question: "Where did they live?" Put the answer in the empty box.

Detail Question	Answer
Who is the passage about?	Native Americans
Where did they live?	
When did they first come in contact with European settlers?	early 1600s
What did they use?	bows and arrows

The answer, North America, is in the first sentence of the paragraph. When you read, try to notice names, places, dates, and other facts. If a *who, what, why, where, when,* and *how* word is used in a TABE question, underline it. Then look back at the paragraph to find the answer.

Test Example

Read the paragraph. Answer the question by circling the letter of the best answer.

> Native Americans of the Plains got most of what they needed to survive from the buffalo. Buffalo meat provided food. The hide was used to make teepees and clothing. Tools and weapons were made from bones, and rope was made from hair.

TABE Strategy

Underline the word *what* in the question and refer back to the paragraph to find the answer.

1 For what purpose did the Native Americans use buffalo hair?

A to make rope   C to make clothing

B to make teepees   D to make weapons

Practice

Read the passage. Answer the questions by circling the letter of the best answer.

The early Native Americans of the Plains traveled and hunted on foot. When these nomadic tribes moved, they used dogs to pull sleds with their belongings. Families could only own as much as their dogs could pull.

In 1541, Spanish explorers introduced horses to North America. The Native Americans cherished horses. Many Native Americans called horses "sky dogs" in their languages. The Native Americans thought the strange animals were large dogs, sent as a gift from the Great Spirit of the sky.

The introduction of the horse increased the supply of food and improved mobility for the Native Americans. Hunting became more successful with horses. Using horses, hunters could keep up with a moving herd of buffalo. A man with a fast horse could bring home more buffalo to feed his family. Horses could also pull heavier loads than the dogs could pull. Families could now own larger teepees and fill them with more supplies.

1 According to the passage, who brought horses to North America?

A the sky dogs

B the Great Spirit

C the Native Americans

D the Spanish explorers

2 What method of travel did the early Native Americans use?

F They walked.

G They rode dogs.

H They rode horses.

J They rode in wagons.

3 According to the passage, why were horses cherished?

A They were beautiful creatures.

B They were brought by the Spanish.

C They improved hunting and traveling.

D They were thought to be related to dogs.

4 According to the passage, how were horses used?

F to train dogs

G to pull supplies

H to guard the teepees

J to carry the children

5 Which of the following probably explains why horses were called "sky dogs"?

A They liked to chase dogs.

B They were compared to birds in the sky.

C They were believed to have fallen from the sky.

D They resembled dogs and were thought to be a gift from a sky spirit.

Check your answers on page 88.

Lesson 9 Sequence

The sequence of a story is the order in which the events happen. Knowing how to tell what comes first, second, third, and so on will help you to understand how a story unfolds. Most stories begin with the first event in the sequence of events and end with the last event. Sequence words can help you to understand the order in which events happen within a story. The TABE will have questions in which you will need to determine the sequence of events in a story.

Example **Read the paragraph. As you read, pay attention to the underlined sequence words that show the order of events. Underline the event that happened after Lance Armstrong won the Iron Kids Triathlon.**

> Lance Armstrong was a natural athlete at an early age. At age 13, he won the Iron Kids Triathlon. <u>Then</u> he became a professional triathlete at age 16. Although Lance was a strong runner and swimmer, his favorite thing to do was race a bike. <u>After</u> graduating from high school, he decided to devote all of his time and energy to competitive cycling. In 1992, Lance finished 14th in the Olympic Games. Many wins <u>later</u>, he was named American Male Cyclist of the Year.

Did you underline the sentence that says Lance Armstrong became a professional triathlete? The sentence, "Then he became a professional athlete", comes right after the sentence, "At age 13, he won the Iron Kids Triathlon." The word *then* is a sequence word that tells you that the next event is about to follow.

Test Example

Read the paragraph. As you read, pay attention to the sequence words that indicate the order of events. Answer the question by circling the letter of the best answer.

> Lance's victories came to a sudden stop in 1996. He was told he had cancer. Lance was only 25 years old. After he got the bad news, he started an aggressive treatment program. First, he had three surgeries. Then he had chemotherapy. During the ordeal, Lance never gave up his cycling dreams. He missed the 1997 cycling season, but finally returned to the sport a year later.

Hint

When you read, look for sequence words such as *first, next, then, after, later,* and *finally.*

1 When did Lance have chemotherapy?

   A after he had three surgeries

   B when he returned to the sport

   C after he was treated for cancer

   D during the 1997 cycling season

1 **A** Chemotherapy was the second part of Lance's treatment program for cancer. According to the paragraph, he had chemotherapy *after* he had three surgeries. Option B is not correct because Lance returned to the sport of cycling *after* he was treated with chemotherapy. Option C is not correct because the chemotherapy was part of his cancer treatment, not something he did after his cancer treatment. Option D is not correct because Lance missed the 1997 cycling season while he was being treated for cancer.

Practice

Read the passage. Answer the questions by circling the letter of the best answer.

Lance Armstrong fought his way through cancer. After his recovery, he was determined to get back into racing. It was a slow, hard battle to get back into shape. First, he had to strengthen his muscles. Then he had to build up his stamina.

Many people thought that he should give up racing altogether, but Lance never quit. He got a lot of help and support from his wife, Kristin, whom he married in 1998. In July of 1999, Lance entered the most famous cycling race of all, the *Tour de France*. To everyone's surprise, he crossed the finish line far ahead of all the other riders. Lance held his arms up high at the moment of victory. He had finally made it to the top of the cycling world.

Later, in October of 1999, Lance and Kristin had a baby. They named him Luke David. Luke inspires Lance as much as Lance inspires people all over the world. Lance tells other cancer survivors, "Maybe I can prove that it's possible to return to a normal life, and maybe I can prove that it's possible to be better than you were before."

1 What happened first?

A Lance got married.

B Lance's baby was born.

C Lance got back into shape for racing.

D Lance won the Tour de France.

2 When did Lance get married?

F July of 1999

G October of 1999

H after he won the Tour de France

J before he won the Tour de France

3 When did Lance get back into shape?

A after his recovery

B before he had cancer

C after his baby was born

D after he won the Tour de France

4 What happened last?

F Lance got married.

G Lance's baby was born.

H Lance got back into shape.

J Lance won the Tour de France.

Check your answers on pages 88–89.

Lesson 10 | Stated Concepts

A stated concept is an expressed idea, opinion, or reason. It can explain why an event happens or why someone behaves in a certain way. Stated concepts can also tell a person's position on a topic. Understanding stated concepts can help you decide whether or not you agree with a particular point of view.

Example Read the paragraph below. A stated concept is underlined. Why are the makers of BGH so proud of their product? _____

_____

> Today, some milk and dairy products are made with a human-made growth hormone called BGH. This hormone is injected into cows. <u>The companies that make and sell BGH boast about how farmers who use their product have increased profits. The makers of BGH claim that it increases a cow's milk production by as much as 10 to 30 percent, while the amount of food the cow eats goes up by only 5 to 10 percent.</u>

They say that their product helps farmers boost profits. The answer to the question comes from the last two sentences. The makers of BGH believe that because a cow injected with the growth hormone makes more milk, but doesn't eat a lot more, profits increase.

Some of the answer choices in the TABE may not be *directly* stated in the passage. They may be restated ideas that combine information from more than one sentence in the passage.

Test Example

Read the paragraph. Answer the question by circling the letter of the best answer.

> When she became pregnant with her daughter, Sasha Miller was concerned that milk made with the help of BGH would cause harmful side effects in her baby. While some thought she was being overly careful, Sasha stood firm and permanently switched to organic milk, which does not come from cows injected with BGH. Is she right to boycott BGH dairy products? Do the hormones pose serious health risks? Sasha is joined by hundreds of other health-conscious consumers who think so. Together, they are the driving force behind sales of natural and organic products. This is now the fastest-growing segment of the food industry.

1 Which of these best describes Sasha's feelings about BGH milk?

   A She likes the flavor of BGH milk.

   B She fears that BGH could cause harm to her baby's health.

   C She is concerned about how boycotts will affect the milk industry.

   D She worries that her baby will like BGH milk better than organic milk.

1 B Sasha is concerned about the health risks of BGH. She worries that it might cause harmful side effects in her baby. The paragraph does not mention Sasha's concern about BGH milk's flavor or taste (options A and D). Sasha is boycotting BGH milk (option C).

Practice

Read the article. Answer the questions by circling the letter of the best answer.

BGH: Who Stands to Profit

Fifteen percent of American dairy cows are now injected with a growth hormone called BGH. In medical studies, BGH has been linked to cancer and other diseases in dairy cows. Even though Canada has banned the use of BGH, the United States has approved its use. Do the risks of BGH outweigh the possible benefits?

If BGH does what it advertises to do, it should increase farmers' production more than costs. Therefore, it will also raise profits. However, if BGH raises milk production, it will make the country's milk surplus grow. This country *already* produces a surplus of milk. The price of milk will drop and force many small dairy farms out of business, unless the government steps in to help.

Does more milk equal more money? It does for a select few. Obviously, the makers and sellers of BGH get the biggest payoff from BGH sales. They make an estimated $300 to $500 million each year from sales of BGH. Because the United States already produces more milk than it can use, the government will have to buy the additional milk at an estimated cost to taxpayers of $200 million or more per year.

1 According to the article, who would benefit the most from the use of BGH?

A taxpayers

B small dairy farmers

C the federal government

D companies that make and sell BGH

2 Which of these expresses a stated relationship between BGH and dairy cows?

F BGH makes cows more fertile.

G BGH makes cows more aggressive.

H Cows injected with BGH have cancer more often.

J BGH decreases the milk production of dairy cows.

3 According to the article, how will taxpayers be affected by the use of BGH?

A They will pay a lot less for milk.

B They will enjoy increased health benefits.

C They will get more choices of milk brands.

D They will have to help offset the costs of a milk surplus.

4 Which of these best represents Canada's position on BGH?

F Canada has banned the use of BGH.

G Canada's dairy farms do not have a need for BGH.

H Canada has made BGH legal to use in only some dairy cows.

J Canada's farmers can choose whether or not to use BGH.

Check your answers on page 89.

Read this article from a weightlifting magazine. Answer the questions by circling the letter of the best answer.

Shock Training

You finally have a weight-training program and you've stuck with it for a while. Now what? If you want to keep seeing results, it's time for a change in your routine. Before now, you probably thought that building muscle was all about finding and sticking with the perfect workout, right? Well, it's not that simple. Building muscle is about having a few regular routines, and trying a new one every now and then.

Bodybuilders are very familiar with working through "plateaus." It's common to plateau by doing the same thing again and again. You can try increasing the amount of weights you use, but that is only part of the solution. Shock training can help you move past a plateau.

Shock training "shocks" your muscles in order to stimulate more growth. What can you do to change your regular routine? If you typically use the leg press once every five days, try using it once every ten days. Also try replacing bench presses with some flies, or adding free weights into your weight-lifting circuit. Adding an occasional variation can help give your muscles just the boost they need.

Of course, always discuss any exercise program with your doctor before beginning. 🍃

---

1 According to this article, how could you move past a "plateau"?

  A Run 3 miles a week.

  B Lift lighter weights.

  C Change your routine.

  D Do more repetitions.

2 What does the author suggest doing if you normally use the leg press once every five days?

  F Add more weight.

  G Stop using the leg press.

  H Try using free weights instead.

  J Try using the leg press once every ten days.

3 Which of these explains why bodybuilders sometimes stop seeing results?

  A They use the weight-lifting circuit.

  B They try new workouts.

  C They eat more fatty foods.

  D They stick to the same workouts.

4 Which of these is considered an example of "shock training"?

  F adding more carbohydrates to your diet

  G replacing the bench press with some flies

  H inviting a friend to help you with your workout

  J doing the same routine every other day for two weeks

Read this passage about Arnold Schwarzenegger, a famous bodybuilder. Answer the questions by circling the letter of the best answer.

Arnold Schwarzenegger was born in Austria on July 30, 1947. His father encouraged Arnold and his brother to play sports. He once told Arnold that he wanted him to be a star soccer player. Arnold tried to please his father, and he became a very good soccer player at school. Yet, his brother remained a far better player. Arnold was upset because his father never praised his best efforts. Arnold dropped out of soccer and started lifting weights at a local gym. At age 13, Arnold had already decided that he wanted to be the best bodybuilder in the world.

Soon Arnold was training seven days a week at the gym. One Sunday the gym was closed, but this didn't stop Arnold. He broke into the gym so that he could work out. Arnold didn't seem to mind that the heat was not on and it was the middle of winter. He kept on training.

When Arnold turned 18, he joined the Austrian army for mandatory service. Arnold's parents hoped that the army would rid their son's passion for bodybuilding, but Arnold proved to be tougher than they had ever thought. One time he secretly left the army camp to compete in the Junior Mr. Europe Bodybuilding Competition. He won the title. Then, in 1966, Arnold entered the Mr. Universe Competition, where he won second place. The following year, he entered again and won first place. At the age of 20, Arnold became the youngest Mr. Universe in history. He had accomplished his dream.

5 According to the passage, which of these best describes Arnold's reaction to his father?

A He was unhappy because his father didn't praise him.

B He was joyful that his father supported and encouraged him.

C He was angry that his father didn't come to his competitions.

D He was amused to learn that his father like bodybuilding too.

6 When did Arnold win first place in the Mr. Universe Competition?

F in 1966

G when he was 18 years old

H when he was 20 years old

J before he joined the army

7 What did Arnold do once when the gym was closed?

A He went home.

B He waited outside.

C He broke in to train.

D He went to another gym.

8 Where was Arnold born?

F Germany

G France

H Austria

J Belgium

Check your answers on page 89.

Lesson 11 — Character Aspects

Character aspects are personal traits or inner qualities of a person. Being able to identify the character aspects of the people you read about helps you to understand what causes them to act or behave in a certain way.

Example — **Read this paragraph. How does Carlos feel about this homeless family?** _____

> Carlos Ramirez started The Goodwill Lodge Homeless Shelter in 1987. He got the idea one day when he was stopped on the sidewalk by a woman asking for money. He had seen homeless people on the street before, but there was something different about this woman. From behind her long, torn coat, peered the sad eyes of a young child. Carlos thought of his son at home—safe, warm, and well-fed. Would he walk away if this were his own child?

Did you write that Carlos felt compassion and concern for the homeless family? The paragraph tells you that the woman reminded Carlos of his son. He asked himself if he would walk away if his own child was cold and hungry. Carlos was so deeply moved by this experience that he opened a homeless shelter to help make a difference.

To understand a person's inner qualities and inner drives:
- Look at his or her words, behaviors, and actions.
- Pay attention to how his or her feelings are described.
- Notice the events she or he is involved in.

Test Example

Read this paragraph. Answer the question by circling the letter of the best answer.

> There were more than forty children and adults living at The Goodwill Lodge during the first month that it opened. Carlos quickly learned the names of all of the people. He spent time taking care of children while their parents went to look for work. He liked listening to the stories that people told about their lives. Carlos was glad that they finally had a place to stay and feel safe.

TABE Strategy

As you read, circle "feeling words" such as *proud, angry, sad, joyous,* and *thankful.*

1 In this paragraph, how can Carlos's feelings toward the people living at the homeless shelter be described?

   A He was tired of listening to their stories.

   B He was disappointed that they didn't have jobs.

   C He was happy that they had a place to sleep and eat.

   D He was frustrated because it was hard to learn more than forty names.

1 C The last sentence said that Carlos "was glad" that the people living at the shelter had a place to stay. Option A is incorrect because it said that he *liked* listening to their stories. Option B is incorrect because the paragraph didn't mention that Carlos was upset or disappointed. Option D is incorrect because learning their names came *quickly* to Carlos.

Practice

Read the letter that a woman sent to the homeless shelter. Answer the questions by circling the letter of the best answer.

> Dear Carlos,
>
> My name is Linda Conners. You might remember me. You used to joke around with me while I stayed at The Goodwill Lodge.
>
> I lost my job at the fish factory about a year ago. I couldn't afford to pay my rent. So, I sold all my furniture and packed up whatever I could fit in my car. There were many cold nights that I spent huddled in the back seat hoping that no one would notice me. It was one of the scariest times in my life.
>
> Then I heard about your shelter. I stayed at The Goodwill Lodge for six weeks. Finally I found a new job as a waitress at a nearby seafood restaurant. Soon I had enough money to pay for the first month's rent on a one-bedroom apartment. I was happy to get back on my feet again.
>
> Thank you for having the vision to open The Goodwill Lodge Homeless Shelter. The kindness that you showed me will never be forgotten.
>
> Thankfully yours,
> Linda Conner

1 From reading the letter, you could say that Carlos and Linda both

A like to laugh

B like to eat fish

C wanted to get jobs

D have trouble sleeping

2 Which of these is probably true about Linda?

F She sold her furniture because she wanted a new bedroom set.

G She could joke around only when her life was going smoothly.

H She turned to the shelter because she didn't want to keep sleeping in her car.

J She went to the shelter because she was ill.

3 In the letter, how can Linda's feelings toward The Goodwill Lodge be described?

A She is relieved that The Goodwill Lodge is no longer open.

B She is afraid of the people who stay at The Goodwill Lodge.

C She is disappointed that she couldn't stay at The Goodwill Lodge longer.

D She is grateful that The Goodwill Lodge was there when she needed a place to stay.

Check your answers on pages 89–90.

Main Idea

The main idea is the general topic of a passage. When you read, it is important to know the basic meaning of what you are reading. The TABE will ask you to identify the main idea of short excerpts or passages.

Example **Read the paragraph. What is it mostly about?** _____

_____

> In 1943, the aqua-lung was invented. The aqua-lung is carried on a scuba diver's back. It allows a diver to breathe enough air to stay underwater for several hours. Before the invention of the aqua-lung, divers had to breathe using long air hoses that reached the water's surface.

The first sentence of this paragraph tells what the paragraph is about. It is called a *topic sentence*. A topic sentence "sums up" or gives a short summary of a paragraph's main idea. Often the topic sentence is the first or the last sentence of a paragraph.

Did you write that the paragraph is about the invention of the aqua-lung? The paragraph explains what an aqua-lung is and what it does.

Test Example

Read this paragraph. Answer the question by circling the letter of the best answer.

> Masks, fins, and snorkels are three basic but important pieces of equipment that a diver needs. To see clearly underwater, divers use a mask. They use fins to move quickly through the water. To be able to swim face-down, a diver needs a snorkel. This makes swimming much easier than lifting the head up to breathe. Before buying any other scuba equipment, a diver should first purchase a good mask, snorkel, and fins.

TABE Strategy

To get the main idea of a passage, try underlining the first and last sentence of every paragraph. Re-read them in order. This will provide you with a short summary of the passage.

1   Which of these is the best title for this excerpt?

    A "Diving in the Caribbean"

    B "How to Use A Snorkel"

    C "Learning to Scuba Dive"

    D "Basic Diving Equipment"

> **1** **D** The excerpt is about the three basic pieces of equipment needed to scuba dive: a mask, fins, and a snorkel. The paragraph doesn't mention *where* to dive (option A). The paragraph doesn't go into detail about *how to use* the equipment (option B). The paragraph doesn't tell *how* to scuba dive (option C).

This passage is about a famous underwater explorer. Read the passage and answer the questions by circling the letter of the best answer.

Jacques Cousteau was born in France in 1910. Ever since he was a child, Jacques loved the water. He knew that he always wanted to be near the ocean.

In 1933 Cousteau joined the French Navy. It was during his service that he began his underwater explorations. In 1937 Cousteau married Simone Melchoir, and they had two sons. Two years after their marriage, Cousteau fought for the French in World War II. During the war, he still found time to continue his underwater work. In 1943, he helped invent the aqua-lung, which allowed a diver to stay underwater for several hours. The aqua-lung was used to locate and remove underwater enemy mines.

In 1951 Cousteau bought a ship to further his explorations. He named it *Calypso*. To pay for his trips on *Calypso*, he made underwater films and wrote many books about ocean life. He also created a TV show called *The Undersea World of Jacques Cousteau*. This popular show was on television for about nine years.

In 1974 Jacques established The Cousteau Society. It worked to help people understand and protect the water systems of the planet. Cousteau was awarded the Presidential Medal of Freedom in 1985. In 1989 the French honored Cousteau with membership in the French Academy. Jacques Cousteau died in 1997. He will always be remembered for being a great inventor and explorer who helped educate the world about ocean life.

1 What is this passage mostly about?

A a popular TV show about sea animals

B a famous inventor and underwater explorer

C how underwater mines were used in World War II

D a group that helps to educate people about ocean life

2 Which of these is the best title for the excerpt?

F "The Story of the *Calypso*"

G "My Life as an Inventor"

H "Famous French Explorers"

J "The Life of Jacques Cousteau"

3 Which of these best tells about Jacques Cousteau's life?

A He spent his life helping others learn about ocean life.

B He fought bravely in World War II and was a war hero.

C He taught French scuba divers how to use the aqua-lung.

D He was a devoted family man who had a wife and two sons.

4 When was the Cousteau Society formed?

F 1910

G 1933

H 1974

J 1997

Check your answers on page 90.

Lesson 13 Summary and Paraphrase

A summary is a brief report that covers the main points. Being able to sum up what you have read in one or two concise sentences is useful when writing a short report. It is also a useful verbal skill when you want to briefly tell others the main idea of an article or a story. On the TABE you will be asked to choose a summary that re-words the main points of a passage.

Example **Read the paragraph. Write a one-sentence summary of the main points.**

_____

Police dogs play an important role in search and rescue. They are able to locate missing people even when they are hidden from view. A search dog's main tool is its keen sense of smell. Wherever a person goes, he or she leaves behind a scent. A trained dog can follow a particular scent and lead a team of rescuers on the right trail. Because of this ability, dogs are often able to reduce search time, thereby increasing the chances that a person will be found.

The summary is: Search dogs use their keen sense of smell to find missing people.
- A summary is the general idea of a passage.
- A summary is not just a fact taken from the passage.
- A summary usually includes a subject, an action, and an outcome.

Subject	Action	Outcome
search dogs	follow scents	find missing people

Test Example

Read the paragraph. Answer the question by circling the letter of the best answer.

King is a three-year-old golden retriever. He has been trained to search for missing people. On Monday afternoon, King helped to locate a lost hiker. The hiker was last seen leaving for a weekend hiking trip in Green Mountain National Park. King was given a sample of the hiker's clothing to sniff. He used the scent to lead rescuers down a three-mile trail. The hiker was found lying near a stream. He had a broken leg that he got when he fell off a rocky ledge.

TABE Strategy

As you read the passage, underline the _subject, action,_ and _outcome._ Then choose a summary that includes all three.

1 Which of these is a statement about King that a reporter would probably tell on the evening news?

A King has gone through a training program.

B King likes to hike in Green Mountain National Park.

C King, a search dog, led rescuers to a missing hiker in Green Mountain National Park.

D King's sense of smell helps him find missing people.

1 C This summary includes the *subject*: King; the *action*: leading rescuers; and the *outcome*: finding the missing hiker. Options A and D are facts from the paragraph, but they don't sum up the event. The statement in option B is not accurate. The paragraph says that King located a hiker, not that King likes to hike.

Practice

Read the passage. Answer the questions by circling the letter of the best answer.

The list of responsibilities of an animal control worker is long. Animal control workers drive trucks to look for stray animals. When stray animals are captured, workers take them to an animal shelter. At the shelter, workers check animals for tags. They fill out reports about where they found the animals and write descriptions of them. They use the reports to help find a pet's owners.

The invention of the pet microchip has helped to make the job of an animal control worker much easier. This special computer chip carries the pet's personal identification number. Using a microchip reader, the worker can access a database that has the owner's name, address, and telephone number. The chip can't be lost or damaged, and it lasts for an animal's lifetime.

Pets that have microchips get reunited with their owners much faster than pets that do not. Pets that have chips spend less time in animal shelters. Because of pet microchips, animal control workers can spend more time catching stray animals and less time filling out paperwork.

1 Which of these best summarizes the passage?

A Animal control workers are hard to find because of all their responsibilities.

B Pet microchips help animal control workers find a pet's owners without having to write long reports.

C Pet microchips help owners keep their pets safe.

D Pet microchips are small, but they contain important information.

2 Which of these best describes how the pet microchip makes it easier to reunite lost pets with their owners?

F Animal control workers don't need to write long reports.

G The chip can't be lost or damaged and it lasts for an animal's lifetime.

H The microchips have an identification number that allows access to information about pet owners.

J Animal control workers have more time to do their jobs.

3 Which of these best describes the duties and responsibilities of an animal control worker?

A Animal control workers enter information about a pet's owners into a computer database.

B Animal control workers feed and take care of animals.

C Animal control workers monitor the health of the shelter's animals.

D Animal control workers capture stray animals, bring them to a shelter, and try to locate pet owners.

Check your answers on page 90.

Lesson 14   Cause and Effect

The terms *cause* and *effect* are related. A *cause* is a *reason* that leads to an effect. An *effect* is what happens as a *result* of the cause. For example, a hole in the roof could be the cause for water dripping into a house. Being aware of cause-effect relationships helps one better understand why events happen.

Example   **Read the paragraph. How did the 1950s medical studies linking smoking and lung cancer affect the cigarette market?** _____

> Before the 1950s people smoked unfiltered cigarettes. There was no proof that cigarettes were harmful. Cigarette companies spent a lot of money trying to make people believe that cigarettes were fine. But that all changed with the release of the first medical studies linking smoking and lung cancer. One response to these studies was the filter-tip cigarette. The filter was supposed to screen out tar and nicotine, thereby making cigarettes "safer."

The effect was that cigarette companies starting selling filter-tip cigarettes. The paragraph explains that medical studies showed that cigarettes were linked to cancer. Companies added filters to make cigarettes "safer" so people would keep buying them.

Test Example

Read the paragraph. Answer the question by circling the letter of the best answer.

> The problem with filtered cigarettes is that they don't really help smokers take in less nicotine. They might filter out some of the nicotine, but a smoker's body will crave more. It's a physical addiction. A smoker will smoke as many cigarettes as it takes to get the amount of nicotine the body is used to receiving.

1   Which of these best explains why a smoker may inhale twice as many filtered cigarettes as unfiltered ones?

    A   Filtered cigarettes help smokers crave less nicotine.

    B   Filtered cigarettes taste better than unfiltered cigarettes.

    C   Unfiltered cigarettes are more addictive.

    D   More filtered cigarettes need to be smoked to get the amount of nicotine that a smoker's body is used to receiving.

> **TABE Strategy**
>
> Highlight the key words *how* or *why* in TABE questions. Then ask yourself if each answer choice is true, accurate, and answers the exact question.

1   **D** A person may smoke more filtered cigarettes to get enough nicotine. Filtered cigarettes do not help smokers crave less nicotine (option A). The paragraph doesn't mention the taste of cigarettes (option B). Option C is not supported by the paragraph.

Read the passage. Answer the questions by circling the letter of the best answer.

The larynx is the voice box. Cancer can strike in many different parts of the voice box. The typical person who develops throat cancer has a history of smoking.

The treatment of throat cancer depends on how large the tumor is and its location in the voice box. Small cancers can be treated with radiation, laser surgery, or by removing a small part of the voice box. Large tumors often require removal of the entire voice box, as well as radiation.

People who have their entire voice box removed can still communicate by using a special device to help them speak. When the person talks, a mechanical voice is activated.

Cancer of the throat is curable if it is caught early. If you have a lump in your neck that won't go away, you should see a doctor. The best way to prevent this kind of cancer is to quit smoking. Tobacco causes serious damage to the throat. Over time the damage can turn into cancer. If it is not treated, it can spread to other parts of the body and become life-threatening.

1 Which of these best explains why a person might have his or her voice box removed?

A He or she has a history of smoking.

B He or she has a lump on the neck.

C He or she has a large, cancerous tumor on the larynx.

D He or she can no longer communicate with the voice box.

2 How can a person communicate without a voice box?

F He or she can get a new voice box.

G He or she can use a special device that helps with speech.

H He or she can use a computer that has a mechanical voice.

J He or she can get laser surgery to remove cancer from the voice box.

3 According to the passage, how might a lump on a person's neck affect a person's health?

A It could be cancerous.

B It might cause a person to stop breathing.

C It could travel into a person's stomach.

D It could make speaking very difficult.

4 Which of these is the best reason to quit smoking?

F Over time tobacco damage can turn into cancer.

G Cancer can strike in many different parts of the voice box.

H Tobacco can cause serious damage to the throat.

J Smoking is not good for your vocal cords or larynx.

Check your answers on page 90.

Compare and Contrast

Authors often use descriptive language to compare or contrast feelings, people, places, events, and things. Thinking about how an author compares and contrasts will help you to better understand an author's message. It will also help you to get more pleasure and meaning out of what you read. To identify when an author compares and contrasts, look for context clues that describe actions and feelings. Pay attention to what characters say and how they act.

Example **Read the paragraph. How have Jennifer's feelings about moving changed since speaking with her Uncle Diego?** _____

Jennifer started to question whether or not she should move to Florida. Would she be able to find a good job right away? How would she support her son, Tomas, in the meantime? Jennifer paced around the room until she got a phone call from her Uncle Diego in Miami. Jennifer let out a long sigh when she heard the good news. Her uncle wanted her to work at his restaurant.

Context clues about Jennifer's feelings

Jennifer's feelings changed from worried to relieved. At first, Jennifer "paced around the room" because she was worried about not being able to support her son. When her uncle offered her a job, Jennifer "let out a long sigh" because she felt relieved.

Test Example

Read the paragraph. Answer the question by circling the letter of the best answer.

As the holiday season came nearer, Jennifer began to long for familiar traditions. She started to daydream about her old neighborhood in Puerto Rico. She remembered the excitement that surrounded this time of year. Tomas seemed to share Jennifer's homesickness. He pointed to his uncle's guitar and pleaded, "Mama, can we please have a party like we used to in Puerto Rico?"

TABE Strategy

As you read TABE passages, circle the context words that describe actions or feelings.

1 Right before the holiday season, Jennifer and Tomas both

   A felt sick and wanted to rest

   B wanted to go to a guitar concert

   C missed the holiday traditions in Puerto Rico

   D wanted to daydream about Puerto Rico

1 C Jennifer "daydreamed" about and "longed for" holiday traditions. Tomas did too. We know this because he "pleaded" for a holiday party. They weren't sick (option A); they were homesick. They didn't want to go to a guitar concert (option B). They didn't want to daydream about Puerto Rico (option D); they wanted to be there.

Read the passage. Answer the questions by circling the letter of the best answer.

Jennifer sat down on the stoop to talk with her Uncle Diego about how things were going. "Everything is working out better than I ever could have imagined." Still, as she said this, Jennifer's mouth turned down at the corners.

"Then why do you look so sad?" asked Diego.

She began to explain. "The holiday season makes me think of Puerto Rico. One of my favorite times during the holidays is when friends gather in the evening to go from one house to the next, singing traditional songs."

"Yes!" exclaimed Diego. "I remember. In the neighborhood I grew up in, we went from house to house with musical instruments. The best part," Diego went on, "was when we were invited in for food, drinks, and dancing.

"But Jennifer, we stick to traditions here. This neighborhood has its own version of your favorite tradition. We may not sing all the songs that you are used to, but it's still a wonderful party. The singing and dancing usually lasts until the next morning."

An overwhelming sense of peace swept over Jennifer. She realized that didn't have to miss home anymore. Finally she felt as if she were already at home.

1 By the end of the story, how have Jennifer's feelings changed?

A from furious to pleased

B from indifferent to curious

C from proud to embarrassed

D from homesick to comforted

2 From reading the passage, you could say that both Jennifer and Diego

F miss Puerto Rico and wish to return for the holidays

G have fond memories of growing up with the same holiday tradition

H hope to go from house to house to ask neighbors to join a singing group

J know a lot about Puerto Rican history

3 Which of these best summarizes the passage?

A A woman finds a way to go home for the holidays.

B A woman realizes that you can feel at home away from home.

C A woman works hard and saves money.

D A woman finds a way to keep the spirit of her heritage alive.

4 Which of these best explains why Jennifer was homesick?

F She liked singing traditional songs.

G The holiday parties lasted until the morning.

H She didn't like her new home.

J She missed taking part in holiday traditions.

Check your answers on page 90.

A conclusion is what you can determine or infer from given information. Because authors sometimes hint at subtle meanings, readers must piece together information to make conclusions. Understanding the full meaning of an author's message helps you to become more engaged in what you read.

Example   **Read the paragraph. How do salamanders breathe?** _____

> Salamanders live in streams, rivers, ponds, lakes, and moist woodlands. Most salamanders breathe by using gills, just like fish, or by using lungs, just like humans. Some salamanders don't have lungs or gills, but absorb oxygen from water through their skin.

Salamanders breathe using lungs, gills, or through their skin. This can be concluded from the information in the paragraph.

From The Given Information
• The paragraph states that most salamanders breathe with gills or lungs.
• The paragraph states that some salamanders absorb oxygen through their skin.
• "Absorbing oxygen" means the same as breathing.
You Can Make This Conclusion
• Salamanders breathe using lungs, gills, or through their skin.

Test Example

Read the paragraph. Answer the question by circling the letter of the best answer.

> Salamanders are amazing creatures. They swim like eels, using muscles to propel themselves through the water. They can also walk on land by moving one leg at a time. Salamanders are true survivors. They have the ability to shed their tails and grow them back, as well as re-grow other damaged parts of their bodies.

Hint

Carefully put together the facts when making conclusions.

1   What does "salamanders are true survivors" mean?

   A   Salamanders can remain alive without skin.

   B   Salamanders can travel on land and in water.

   C   Salamanders can glide through the water and escape from eels.

   D   Salamanders can re-grow an injured body part.

1   D "Surviving" means staying alive. Their ability to re-grow body parts would help them survive if a body part was hurt. Option A is not mentioned. Being able to travel on land and in water (option B) is not a survival skill. Salamanders can glide like eels, not escape from them (option C).

Read the article. Answer the questions by circling the letter of the best answer.

Salamander Crossing

A new traffic sign has been put up on Henry Street. It's different than any sign you've seen before. It's a sign for a "salamander crossing". The sign marks new salamander-crossing tunnels that have been installed under Henry Street.

For most of the year, salamanders live in a large park on Henry Street. Every spring the salamanders cross Henry Street to get to a pond where they mate and lay their eggs. The journey happens mostly at night, which makes it difficult for drivers to see salamanders crossing the road.

Local residents expressed their relief over the completion of the project. One homeowner said, "I was tired of seeing the little critters getting squashed every spring by careless drivers."

The two tunnels, about twenty feet apart, were built at the salamanders' regular crossing site. Short fences were put up to guide migrating salamanders into the tunnels. Each tunnel has a slot in the top to let in light and to provide the wet conditions that the salamanders need. People who are interested in watching the salamanders migrate can park at the nearby train station.

1 The purpose of the "salamander crossing" is to

A make the road wider for pedestrians, cyclists, and salamanders

B give salamanders a safe way to cross the road and get to the pond

C warn drivers to slow down for the tunnel

D give residents a pathway to the pond to see the salamanders mate

2 Which of these probably happened before the salamander crossing was built?

F Salamanders found a different route to get to the pond.

G Salamanders laid their eggs in puddles by the side of the road.

H Salamanders were crossing the street and getting run over by cars.

J Police officers stopped traffic for the salamanders to cross the road.

3 Why was a sign put up?

A to mark the location where people can watch the migration

B to warn drivers to slow down for salamanders crossing the street

C to mark the location of the pond where the salamanders lay their eggs

D to warn drivers to slow down for children

4 Which of these details from the article best shows how residents feel about the salamander crossing?

F Slots were put on the tunnels to let light and moisture in.

G Residents can park at the train station to watch the migration.

H One resident is relieved the salamanders are not getting squashed.

J The two tunnels are built twenty feet apart.

Check your answers on page 91.

Lesson 17 Supporting Evidence

Supporting evidence is information that backs up a statement. It is important to have evidence that supports your position or statement. As a result, what you say is more believable. The TABE will ask you to choose a statement that has plenty of supporting evidence to back it up.

Example **Read the paragraph. Find two facts from the paragraph to support this statement: Annie Oakley was good at shooting a gun.**

Fact 1: _____

Fact 2: _____

As a child, Annie Oakley learned to shoot wild animals for food. Her career as a sharpshooter started at age 17 when she beat the famous gunslinger, Frank E. Butler at a competition in Cincinnati, Ohio. The two eventually married and performed with the Buffalo Bill Show for 17 years.

Fact 1: Annie shot wild animals for food. Fact 2: She beat a famous gunslinger during a shooting contest. These two facts from the paragraph can be used to back up, or support, the statement, "Annie Oakley was good at shooting a gun."

Test Example

Read the paragraph. Answer the question by circling the letter of the best answer.

The American West produced many exciting heroes and legends, but none were as entertaining as Annie Oakley. One time she shot a cigarette from the hand of a prince. At thirty paces she could slice a playing card in half. It was said that she could even "scramble" eggs in midair.

TABE Strategy

Read each answer choice. Cross off the answer choices that are not supported by facts from the passage.

1 Which of these statements is best supported by the paragraph?

A Annie Oakley was a legendary sharpshooter.

B Becoming a good shooter requires concentration.

C The most famous marksmen were good at cooking.

D Annie Oakley only shot accurately from a short distance.

1 A Option A is correct because the first sentence describes Annie as a legend of the American West. The paragraph doesn't say that Annie had to concentrate to shoot accurately (option B). It doesn't mention cooking (option C) or say anything about shooting from short distances (option D).

Read the passage. Answer the questions by circling the letter of the best answer.

By the 1930s, tennis had become a popular American sport. However, at that time tennis was mostly dominated by white athletes. Becoming a famous tennis player was still only a dream to African American children.

Althea Gibson changed all that. She became the first African American woman to win a major singles tennis tournament. She was able to show the world that tennis was ready for a change.

Althea was born on a cotton farm in South Carolina, where her parents were sharecroppers. She later moved to Harlem, New York, where she spent most of her childhood. She had trouble in school and often ran away from home.

Developing an interest in tennis was hard because Althea was banned from most public courts because she was African American. She finally learned to play in a public program that brought tennis to children in poor neighborhoods. Her talent and interest in the game helped her win several local tournaments. She won the New York state championship six times from 1944–1950. In 1957, Althea Gibson became the first black player to win at Wimbledon and was named the Associated Press Female Athlete of the year.

1 Which of these facts best supports the statement: You can rise to the top with talent and determination.

A Althea got into trouble at school, but she still graduated.

B Although banned from public courts, Althea still became a great tennis player.

C Even though Althea was born on a farm, she was interested in tennis.

D Even though she was poor, Althea still wanted to play.

2 Which of these statements is best supported by the passage?

F The most famous athletes are tennis players.

G Becoming a tennis player requires access to good coaches.

H A sport may not recognize an athlete right away based on skill alone.

J The talent of a woman is not always recognized in male-dominated sports.

3 By the end of the story, how had Althea's tennis career changed?

A from banned to ignored

B from celebrated to acknowledged

C from acknowledged to ignored

D from banned to celebrated

Check your answers on page 91.

Read the passage. Answer the questions by circling the letter of the best answer.

For years, my father, Manuel Rivera, regularly traveled from town to town. Everything he owned had to be small enough to fit in an oversized army backpack. He worked as a migrant worker. Home was wherever the next harvest was. Moving around to different places suited my father just fine until he met my mother.

"I was used to moving around. It was the life that my parents had and that I followed. Picking fruits and vegetables was what I knew best," he explained. "Then I met your mother and that all changed. I realized that I did not want that kind of life for my children. My dream became to have a home so my own family could have a better life," he told me.

My mother, Helena Garcia, was born in Mexico. When her mother died, Helena and her father moved to the United States. Helena surprised her family when she told them she wanted to become a nurse. She became the first in her family to go to college. She took out a student loan and went to a local community college. During the summers, she picked strawberries to help pay for tuition. That was where she met my father. They got married but owning a home of their own seemed out of reach. Thankfully, an organization called Habitat for Humanity opened a door that may not have opened otherwise. "Habitat helped us to afford a good home where we could raise a family and teach our children the value of education," said my parents.

Using volunteer labor and donated materials, the non-profit group, Habitat for Humanity, built a simple but sturdy house for us. My parents even helped the volunteers build it. When it was done, my mother got a job in nursing and my father worked at a grocery store. It was the first time in his life that he could work around fruits and vegetables without having to move!

1 Which of these is the best title for the passage?

  A "The Story of my Life"

  B "Life as a Migrant Worker"

  C "How our Home Came to Be"

  D "Fruit and Vegetable Farming"

2 Habitat for Humanity probably acquired its name because

  F it provides temporary shelter to migrant workers

  G it provides affordable homes to low-income families

  H it gives opportunities for volunteer work

  J it teaches families how to grow their own fruits and vegetables

3 Which of these best explains why the author's father stopped picking fruits and vegetables?

  A He lost his job.

  B He got a new job in a grocery store.

  C He wanted to learn how to build houses.

  D He didn't want his family to have to move around.

4 From the passage, you can tell that the author's mother wants

  F her children to go to school

  G to own her own strawberry farm

  H to move back in with her parents

  J her husband to pay for her college tuition

5 Which of these best summarizes the last two paragraphs of the passage?

A Habitat for Humanity provided one town with low-cost housing.

B A migrant worker earns a college degree and gets a better paying job.

C Habitat for Humanity helped one family live the dream of having a permanent home.

D A man and a woman get married and raise children in Mexico.

6 By the end of the excerpt, how did the father's feelings change about living the life of a migrant worker?

F from bored to enthusiastic

G from content to dissatisfied

H from appreciative to resentful

J from disenchanted to fulfilled

7 Which of these statements is best supported by the passage?

A Habitat for Humanity builds expensive houses.

B Migrant work is a good way to save money to buy a house.

C The author's mother was used to living in a comfortable home.

D The author's father felt at home wherever he was working.

8 What does the author mean when he says of his father, "It was the first time in his life that he could work around fruits and vegetables without having to move!"?

F This was his father's first job that didn't have to do with food.

G His father wanted to work in a grocery store because he liked traveling.

H His father's new job still involved produce, but it did not require traveling.

J His father's new job required moving fruits and vegetables, not picking them.

9 Which of these is probably true of Manuel Rivera?

A He considers family first.

B He prefers traveling to staying in one place.

C He is used to sleeping on floors.

D He enjoys carpentry.

10 From the passage, you can tell that the author and his parents

F don't know their family history

G appreciate what Habitat for Humanity did for them

H want to go back to being migrant workers

J live in a fancy new house

Check your answers on pages 91–92.

Lesson 18 Fact and Opinion

On the TABE you will have to decide whether a statement in a passage is a fact or an opinion. Facts are based on true information. Opinions are personal views or judgments.

Example **Read the two sentences. Can you tell which one is a fact and which one is**

an opinion? Fact: _____. Opinion: _____.

Sentence 1 Baxter State Park is located in Maine.
Sentence 2 It is one of most beautiful wilderness areas in the northeast.

Sentence 1 is a fact and Sentence 2 is an opinion. The location of Baxter State Park is a fact. However, not everyone might agree that Baxter State Park is one of the most beautiful wilderness areas in the northeast. That is a personal opinion.

When an opinion is expressed, it usually includes descriptive-judgment words. Some examples of descriptive judgment words are in the chart.

Descriptive Judgment Words	
Positive	**Negative**
beautiful	ugly
perfect	flawed
smart	dumb
wonderful	terrible
best	worst

Test Example

Read the paragraph. Answer the question by circling the letter of the best answer.

Baxter State Park is an area that has a history of logging. The first logging was for pine; then spruce; then pulpwood. Baxter was logged from the mid-1800s until 1965. Then logging rights expired and the area was turned into a state-protected preserve. Baxter State Park should be reopened to commercial logging. Keeping the woods from being harvested is a terrible waste of good lumber.

> **TABE** Strategy
>
> As you read TABE passages, highlight descriptive judgment words that may indicate an opinion.

1 Which of these is an <u>opinion</u>?

A The area was logged until 1965.

B The first logging was for pine.

C Keeping the woods from being harvested is a terrible waste of good lumber.

D The logging rights ended and the area was turned into a state park.

> **1 C** The words "terrible waste" indicate an opinion or a personal view of the author. Not everyone would agree. Because option A is a date, it is factual. Option B describes the actual types of wood that were harvested. Option D is a historical statement about how it became a state park.

Read the letter. Answer the questions by circling the letter of the best answer.

Dear Friends and Neighbors:

I am outraged that our state leaders are considering selling commercial logging rights in Baxter State Park. The park is one of Maine's most treasured areas. It was donated by Percival P. Baxter to preserve the area in its natural state. It is an important piece of Maine's natural history that should not be spoiled for profit.

Baxter is home to numerous ponds, lakes, streams, waterfalls and bogs. This all combines to create a magnificent landscape. People from all over New England go hiking and camping in Baxter. The fall foliage in Baxter is spectacular. Taking down the trees would ruin much of the natural beauty.

Many unique plants and wildlife reside within the park. Removing trees would disturb the delicate balance of nature that the animals depend on for their survival.

Many of Maine's forests are under attack from over-harvesting and new development. Let's work together to protect the woods of Baxter from this fate. Baxter State Park should remain in its natural state and continue to be a sanctuary for all to enjoy.

A Concerned Resident of Maine

1 Which of these is an <u>opinion</u> expressed in the letter?

A The fall foliage here is spectacular.

B Baxter is home to numerous ponds.

C Many unique plants and wildlife reside within the park.

D People from all over New England go hiking and camping in Baxter.

2 Which of these sentences from the letter expresses a <u>fact</u>?

F The park is one of Maine's most treasured areas.

G This all combines to create a magnificent landscape.

H Let's work together to protect the woods of Baxter from this fate.

J It was donated by Percival P. Baxter.

3 Which of these is an <u>opinion</u>?

A Baxter State Park is in Maine.

B Ponds can be used for fishing.

C Taking down trees would ruin the natural beauty.

D Baxter State Park has hiking trails.

4 Which of these sentences expresses a <u>fact</u>?

F The park is a wonderful gift that we should protect.

G It is an important piece of Maine's natural history.

H Baxter State Park should remain in its natural state.

J The animals that live in the park include moose, deer, bears, and otters.

Check your answers on page 92.

Apply Passage Elements

Applying information is the same as putting it to specific or practical use. For example, when you are reading a history article, you may be able to apply the information to current events. Or, you may be able to extend the lesson or moral of a story about someone else to your own daily life.

Example **Read the paragraph. What advice would Devon give to friends who are thinking about staying outside during a thunderstorm? _____**

> Devon was up on a ladder fixing a rain gutter when the storm started. He wondered if he should go inside when he heard a loud bang of thunder. He continued to work because he was almost done. That was when the lightning hit. The next thing he knew, Devon was lying on the ground, feeling very dizzy. Luckily he was not too hurt to get up and go into the house to call an ambulance.

Devon would probably advise his friends to go indoors during a thunderstorm. He might tell his friends his story and warn them to stay inside so the same thing does not happen to them.

Test Example

Read the paragraph. Answer the question by circling the letter of the best answer.

> At the hospital, a doctor examined Devon. The doctor explained to Devon that lightning must have hit the ladder he was on. Devon felt lucky to be alive. He decided to spend the rest of the weekend with his children instead of working on the house, as he had planned.

TABE Strategy

As you read the TABE passage, identify and underline or write down the lesson or the moral.

1 With which of these statements would Devon most likely agree?

A A wooden ladder is better than a metal one.

B It is important to repair things before they break.

C Working on a ladder is dangerous.

D Spending time with family is more important than getting the job done.

1 **D** Devon said that he felt "lucky to be alive." That was what made him realize that spending time with his family is more important to him than working on the house. The paragraph didn't mention what kind of ladder Devon was working on (option A). At the end of the paragraph, he is no longer interested in fixing things on the house (option B). The danger was the lightning, not the ladder (option C).

Read the passage. Answer the questions by circling the letter of the best answer

It was noisy inside the dam, but Trisha could still hear the tour guide. "Water from the lake passes through large, fanlike machines called turbines," he shouted. "The water turns those giant fans and creates electricity."

Trisha marveled at all the machinery. Everything was made out of concrete and metal. She walked over to one of the turbines. It was as tall as a house and made of steel. "I'd sure like to climb that thing," she said out loud. "I bet I could make it to the top."

Just then, the tour guide tapped her on the shoulder. "Be careful around that turbine! It's powerful and can be dangerous." The tour guide continued. "Hydro-power is currently the world's largest renewable source of electricity. It accounts for about fifteen percent of the world's electricity and is an inexpensive and clean source of power. The electricity created by this dam lights communities many miles away!"

For a moment, Trisha thought of her life without electricity. "Without electricity, I couldn't watch TV." Her mind raced on. "I couldn't listen to music because the stereo wouldn't work. I couldn't play my new computer game because the computer wouldn't even turn on."

When Trisha's group walked outside again, Trisha looked up at the top of the dam way above her. "One day," she thought, "I'd like to work on a big turbine in a dam."

1 With which of these statements would the tour guide agree?

A Windmills are the best form of alternative energy.

B More hydro-dams should be built around the world.

C Water should not be used for anything except drinking.

D Rivers should not be dammed.

2 At the end of the excerpt, if Trisha heard someone in the next group complaining about having to go on the tour, she would most likely respond by

F talking about her career plans

G ignoring them

H explaining how valuable hydro-dams are to people

J vigorously agreeing with them

3 What advice would the tour guide probably offer to people who are interested in developing alternative forms of energy?

A Water can be used to create an endless supply of power.

B Coal and oil-fueled power plants are inexpensive to build.

C The world has enough renewable sources of energy already.

D Consumers should be taught ways to conserve electricity.

4 From reading the passage, you can tell that Trisha

F is not interested in working in a dam

G values that electricity allows her to use the refrigerator

H is interested in machinery

J doesn't like computer games

Check your answers on page 92.

Lesson 20 Generalizations

When you generalize, you apply information to other situations. Some TABE questions will require you to think beyond what you have read. You must use the information from the passage to generalize and choose the answer that makes the most sense.

Example **Read this paragraph about polio. Should American parents, Nancy and Tom, get their baby vaccinated against polio? _____**

> Polio is a serious disease. There is no cure for it. Therefore, the best way to avoid the disease is prevention. The United States and many other countries are free of polio. However, because of world-wide travel, it is important for people to have immunity to the disease. This will prevent it from spreading and causing an epidemic.

Nancy and Tom *should* get their baby vaccinated against polio. The answer is not directly stated in the paragraph, but it can be generalized from the information given.

Test Example

Read the paragraph. Answer the question by circling the letter of the best answer.

> In the past, polio was common and greatly feared. It left thousands of people dependent on braces, crutches, and wheelchairs. In the 1950s, however, a vaccine against the disease was introduced.

TABE Strategy

First eliminate the answer choices that, based on what you read, don't seem likely or possible.

1 Based on the paragraph, which of these is probably true?

A Polio only affects children.

B Braces were used to help prevent polio.

C Some people affected with polio cannot walk.

D Before 1950, people were not as afraid of contracting polio.

1 C The paragraph states that many people who have had polio use braces, crutches, and wheelchairs. Therefore, polio must affect people's ability to walk. Readers cannot assume that all polio victims are children (option A). Braces are used to help people walk (option B), not to prevent polio. Option D is not correct because people were not as afraid of contracting polio *after* the introduction of the vaccine in 1950.

Read the passage. Answer the questions by circling the letter of the best answer.

When Europeans sailed across the Atlantic Ocean to North America, they brought many things with them. They introduced horses, cows, and oxen to the Native Americans. They also brought diseases. Smallpox was one of the most deadly diseases. It wiped out entire tribes of Native Americans.

The Europeans had already been exposed to smallpox, so they were often protected from catching the disease—or at least from dying from it. But Native Americans had no resistance to smallpox. Many of them died as a result of being exposed to it.

When the Europeans met the Native Americans, the smallpox virus passed from the Europeans' lungs into the lungs of the Native Americans. Smallpox also infected bedding and clothing. As trading began between the two groups, blankets and other goods made their way into the villages, exposing more people to the disease.

With the invention of the steamboat, more trade routes opened and goods were brought into new trading posts. This set the stage for disaster as smallpox was able to reach new victims.

It is estimated that diseases killed between 100,000 to 300,000 Native Americans in the mid-nineteenth century. Smallpox was, by far, the biggest killer. It greatly reduced the Native-American population and changed their culture forever.

1 The invention of the steamboat made

A travel more difficult

B buffalo hides more expensive for buyers

C infected blankets more available to isolated tribes

D trading more confrontational between fur traders and blanket traders

2 Based on the passage, which of these is probably true?

F The Europeans were all vaccinated against smallpox.

G Smallpox is a disease that was not native to North America.

H Smallpox helped Native American culture grow and expand.

J The Atlantic Ocean prevented many diseases from being brought to America.

3 How can Native Americans living today be protected against diseases?

A They can get vaccinations.

B They can stop using blankets.

C They can wear face masks for protection.

D They can stay in America and never go to Europe.

Check your answers on page 92.

Authors write for different reasons or purposes. If you are aware of the intended purpose of what you are reading, you can judge how useful the information is to you.

Example **Read this letter. Why did the author write it?** _____

> To the manager of Berkshire Appliances,
>
> I am looking for a job. I am very handy with tools and I can fix almost anything. I even know how to repair refrigerators and air conditioners. Can you please tell me if your company is hiring right now?
>
> Sincerely,
>
> *Greg Davis*
>
> Greg Davis

The author wrote the letter to find out if Berkshire Appliances has any job openings. If you were the manager of an appliance store and you needed a repairperson, this letter might be very useful to you.

Test Example

Read this help-wanted advertisement. Answer the question by circling the letter of the best answer.

1 The purpose of writing this advertisement was probably to

  A ask a store manager if they need an appliance repairperson

  B find a qualified person to work as an appliance repairperson

  C let homeowners know whom to call if they need their appliances fixed

  D persuade potential employers to contact an appliance repairperson who is looking for a job

> **APPLIANCE REPAIRPERSON NEEDED**
> Repairperson needed to install and repair gas meters, ranges, heaters, air conditioners, and refrigerators in homes and businesses. Applicants must be able to use rulers, pipe cutters, wrenches, and other tools. Responsibilities include collecting money for monthly bills or overdue payments. Apply in person at Berkshire Appliances.

1 B The advertisement is intended to let people know that there is a job opening for an appliance repairperson. It lists the skills required for the job as well as a description of the job responsibilities.

Read this article. Answer the questions by circling the letter of the best answer.

Here are three steps you can use to track down jobs and find the one that is just right for you.

STEP 1: Look for a Position First you have to know what it is that you are good at and enjoy doing. Look for positions that match your interests, skills, and abilities. Check every resource. Look in the classified section of local newspapers. Look for job postings on the Internet. Ask friends and family members if they know of any job openings in your field.

Step 2: Prepare Your Resume A resume showcases your skills and work experience. Buying a book on how to write a resume is a good investment. Make sure to list skills and qualifications that match the position you are applying for. Remember that you are selling yourself, so it is important to look qualified on paper!

Step 3: Get Ready for Your Interview Before an interview, find out as much as you can about the organization or company. Find out what skills they look for in applicants. Read up on information about them and talk to current employees. Ask intelligent questions during the interview. The idea is to be prepared. After the interview is over, be sure to follow up with a phone call or letter to say thank you. This will impress your potential boss and show that you are truly interested in the position.

1 The author's purpose in writing this article is probably to

A tell a story about finding a job

B teach people how to write a good resume

C challenge employers to create more jobs

D describe how to search for a job

2 The writer probably wants readers to

F agree with a point of view

G find a job that will be a good match

H get more involved in volunteer positions

J tell people how to locate the classified section of the newspaper

3 Which of these is the best title for the passage?

A "Three Tips for Successful Job Hunting"

B "A Resume Showcases Your Skills and Work Experience"

C "Get the Benefits That are Right for You"

D "How to Conduct Yourself in an Interview"

4 Which of these statements is best supported by the passage?

F If you know your strengths, you can find the right job for you.

G The more you prepare, the more effective your job search will be.

H A well-written resume will get the attention of potential employers.

J Tracking down opportunities is as easy as 1, 2, 3.

Check your answers on page 92.

Lesson 22 Point of View

A person's point of view is the way in which he or she sees or judges a situation. If you can identify an author's point of view, you can decide whether you agree or disagree.

Example **Read the paragraph. What is the author's point of view on tax increases?**

_____

> There have been too many tax increases this year. This city's residents pay the highest taxes in the state. Instead of raising taxes to help pay for city expenses, the city should cut services to reduce the cost to taxpayers.

The author is against tax increases. You may have the same opinion about tax increases. However, you might disagree with the author's point of view. The chart below lists phrases that are often used to introduce an opinion.

These phrases usually introduce a point of view.	
_I_ think. . .	_I_ do not think. . .
_I_ believe. . .	_I_ do not believe. . .
_I_ support. . .	_I_ do not support. . .
_I_ agree with. . .	_I_ disagree with. . .
_I_ would like. . .	_I_ would not like. . .

Test Example

Read the paragraph. Answer the question by circling the letter of the best answer.

> The city should not cut back the services it provides. This city is known for its good schools, excellent road maintenance, and reliable trash pick-up. Residents should chip in and pay a little more in order for the quality of services to continue.

TABE Strategy

As you read TABE passages, look for the word _should_. This could introduce a point of view or opinion.

1 The author of the paragraph would probably

   A not want to pay any more money for services

   B help pay for a share of the increase in service costs

   C like to see people paying privately for their trash pick-up

   D rather see cuts in school budgets than pay more taxes

> **1** **B** The author believes that residents should help pay for the increase in service costs. The author does think that people should pay more money (option A). If everyone "chips in" then people wouldn't have to pay for trash pick-up (option C). The author would rather see tax increases than school cutbacks (option D).

Read the two letters. Answer the questions by circling the letter of the best answer.

Letter A

School buses provide a service just like public transit does. It is time that people start paying just like the riders of public transit do.

A lot of districts have started charging transportation fees. It is expensive to pay for transportation across an entire district. Fees would help offset the costs. They would cover drivers' salaries and bus maintenance.

I believe that families who send their children to school on the bus should also pay for the cost of transportation. There is nothing wrong with making parents pay for services their children use.

Letter B

Many families depend on school buses to take their children back and forth to school. Some people have no other alternatives. They live too far away for their child to walk or ride a bike. Many do not have flexible enough work hours to be able to drop off and pick up their child on time.

It's not right to charge fees for school transportation. The taxes people pay should cover their kids' ride to school. Not everyone can afford to pay a fee. Some things in life, such as having a way to get to school, are meant to be free.

1 The writer of Letter A probably would

A agree that public school bus users should pay bus fares

B support people who refuse to pay their child's school bus fee

C help cities and towns finance the costs of school transportation

D like to see every family help pay for school transportation

2 The writer of Letter B probably would

F be willing to pay public school tuition

G help to organize car pools so that buses wouldn't be necessary

H want cities and towns to cover the costs of school transportation

J support a tax increase to cover the costs of school buses

3 The writer's purpose in writing Letter A is probably to

A give information about a subject

B report news

C express a personal opinion

D tell a story

4 Which of these sentences from Letter B expresses a fact?

F Many families depend on school buses.

G The taxes people pay should cover their kids' ride to school.

H It's not right to charge fees for school transportation.

J Some things in life, such as having a way to get to school, are meant to be free.

Check your answers on page 93.

Lesson 23 — Style Techniques

Authors and writers use different style techniques to convey messages. The techniques used depend on the type of information the author is trying to express. Being familiar with different style techniques will help you to appreciate what you read and help you in your own writing.

Example   Read the paragraph. How does the author try to convince readers to

donate blood? _____

> We all know giving blood helps others, but did you know donating blood is also a healthy habit for yourself? Before donating blood, everyone must pass a physical exam. I was surprised to learn that I had dangerously high blood pressure. Donating blood helped me to be aware of a problem before it had a chance to take my life!

The author described an example and used a personal testimony to convince readers to donate blood. The box below outlines some common style techniques authors use.

Style Technique	What It Is	Example
Concrete Example	a real instance or time that something happened	finding out you have high blood pressure during a physical exam
Exaggerated Details	an overstatement; describing something as greater than it is	The news was so shocking that he tumbled off his chair and almost had a heart attack!
Personal Testimony	when someone testifies or swears to something	"Donating blood made me aware of a problem before it had a chance to take my life!"
Expert Testimonial	when an expert testifies or swears to something	The nurse said, "Getting regular physical exams can mean the difference between life and death."

Test Example

Read the paragraph. Answer the question by circling the letter of the best answer.

> Not paying attention to maintaining your health can cause you major pain and suffering. If you don't go to your doctor for regular physical exams, you could end up getting extremely sick. You might have undiagnosed health problems that will make you deathly ill! If you don't go to the doctor, you only have yourself to blame if you get sick!

Hint

As you read, think about how the author makes a point more convincing or compelling.

1   Which of these techniques does the writer use to describe what could happen to someone who doesn't seek regular medical care?

A   personal testimony

B   exaggerated details

C   concrete example

D   testimonial from an expert

1 B The author uses overstated details to describe what could happen to someone who doesn't seek regular medical care. The description wasn't a real example (option C) or an experience that happened to the author (option A). An expert was not quoted or referred to in this paragraph (option D).

Practice

Read the passage. Answer the questions by circling the letter of the best answer.

During pregnancy, a baby's umbilical cord is the lifeline between it and its mother. After a baby is born, umbilical-cord blood can be a lifeline to others, too. It can be used for medical treatments that can help save the life of a child or adult who has leukemia (bone marrow cancer). I know, because I am a leukemia survivor who benefited from this life-saving technique.

The blood in the umbilical cord helps a baby to grow. It has special cells called "stem cells." Stem cells are also found in bone marrow. Umbilical cords, usually discarded at birth, can help give someone a second chance at life. They are useful in the treatment of leukemia and nearly forty other life-threatening diseases.

Unlike bone marrow, umbilical-cord blood is easy to collect. It can be taken right after birth without risk to the child or mother. It is a simple and painless procedure.

By donating umbilical-cord blood, mothers and their newborn babies can become heroes. And, because there are more than 10,000 babies born in the United States every day, there are at least 10,000 possibilities of hope for leukemia patients around the world.

1 What was the "lifeline" that the author referred to?

A a rope used to save accident victims

B a tube used to give blood to hospital patients

C a life-saving treatment

D a device used to remove the umbilical cord from a newborn baby

2 Which of these techniques does the writer use to convince readers?

F personal testimony

G exaggerated details

H concrete example

J testimonial from an expert

3 What was the "10,000 possibilities of hope" the author referred to?

A the number of stem cells in one umbilical cord

B different kinds of bone marrow

C the babies who are born every day

D all of the possible cancer treatments

4 What was the "second chance at life" the author referred to?

F the possibility of a cure for a deadly disease

G a medicine

H a way of harvesting bone marrow

J a way of giving birth to a baby

Check your answers on page 93.

Lesson 24 Genre

Everything that you read can be classified into a genre, or type of writing. Each genre of writing has its own unique purpose and audience. Being familiar with the different types of writing will help you know where to look for certain information in a library or bookstore. It is also helpful to know about all of the possible reading choices that exist when you read for pleasure.

Example **Read the paragraph. In what type of book would you find a paragraph like this?** _____

The American Civil War was fought between April 1861 and April 1865. It is one of the most studied conflicts in modern history. The roots of the war go back to the birth of the nation.

A paragraph like this could be found in a history textbook. The different genres of writing generally fall into one of two categories: *fiction* or *non-fiction*. The charts below describe these two categories.

Fiction	Not true; usually tells a story
Formats	Books, novels, and magazine articles

Genres	Themes/Characteristics
Mystery	detectives, secrets, crime
Romance	love, relationships
Science fiction	outer space, the future
Western	cowboys, horses
Fantasy	fantastical fairy tales

Non-Fiction	True; usually gives factual information
Formats	Books, textbooks, magazine articles, news articles and editorials, journals, essays, and reports

Genres	Themes/Characteristics
Informational	topic related
Biographies	about a person's life
Personal narrative	about the author's life

Test Example

Read the paragraph. Answer the question by circling the letter of the best answer.

The starting pitcher is expected to begin the season on the disabled list. He is recovering from a shoulder injury. The coaches hope to have him back in play by next weekend's game.

TABE Strategy

Label what you read as *fiction* or *non-fiction*.

1 This paragraph would most likely be found in

A a mystery novel

B a math textbook

C a daily newspaper

D an essay about the history of baseball

1 **C** The paragraph is a sports article about a baseball player. The paragraph is non-fiction, so it would not be a novel (option A). The topic is not related to math (option B). An essay about baseball history would not be specific about one player's minor injury (option D).

For numbers 1 and 2, read the passage. Then answer the questions by circling the letter of the best answer.

What do food, clothing, wood, and water all have in common? They all come directly or indirectly from soil. Most of the food we eat comes from the soil. The fibers we use to make some of our clothing comes from plants that are grown in soil. Wood comes from trees that hold their roots in soil. Much of the groundwater that we drink is pumped up from the soil.

Soil is a very complex substance that forms very slowly over time. An inch of soil can take hundreds of years to form. If you were to investigate soil under a microscope, you would marvel at the amount of life it contains. A whole ecosystem exists in soil.

1 This passage would most likely appear in

A a cooking magazine

B a science fiction book

C a newspaper editorial

D an introductory text on earth science

2 To find out how to create the best soil for growing vegetables, you would look in

F a daily newspaper

G an article in a gardening magazine

H an advanced textbook on insects that live in the soil

J a novel about a farming community

For numbers 3 and 4, read the passage. Then answer the questions by circling the letter of the best answer.

A disturbance in soil, such as cultivation or adding chemicals, changes the balance of the ecosystem. A change in the soil structure can harm the organisms and animals that live in it. Any change in the soil is reflected in the plants and animals, which are the first to suffer when humans change its composition.

People need to look after and care for soil. Although it is continually being formed, the rate of formation is very slow. This makes it a non-renewable resource. Soil is not just dirt; it is an essential part of the environment. Without healthy soil, we cannot survive.

3 The author's purpose in writing this passage is probably to

A give information about a subject

B report news

C entertain

D tell a story

4 Which of these sentences from the passage expresses an opinion?

F A change in the soil structure can harm the organisms and animals that live in it.

G People need to look after and care for soil.

H A disturbance in soil changes the balance of the ecosystem.

J Soil is a non-renewable resource.

Check your answers on page 93.

Read the passage. Answer the questions by circling the letter of the best answer.

Maya Angelou is best known for her book, *I Know Why the Caged Bird Sings,* which was published in 1970. This book tells the story of Maya's own experiences as an African American girl growing up during the Great Depression. It is a story which illustrates that obstacles in life can be overcome with strength and determination.

The story begins with Maya Angelou's birth on April 4, 1928 in St. Louis, Missouri. Her birth name was Marguerite Johnson. She later changed her name to Maya, the nickname her brother gave her as a child. Angelou was her first husband's family name.

When she was three years old, Maya's parents divorced, and she was sent with her brother to live with their grandmother in Arkansas. Maya learned many important life lessons from her grandmother, whom she lovingly called "Momma." Although Maya often dreamed of waking up to see her nappy black hair transformed into long, blonde hair, Momma taught Maya to have pride in herself.

After five years, Maya and her brother were sent back to live with their mother. Things took a turn for the worse when, at age eight, Maya was abused by her mother's boyfriend. The trauma she felt caused her to stop speaking for almost five years. Then Maya moved back to Arkansas, where a woman named Mrs. Flowers helped her rebuild her confidence.

The story ends with the birth of Maya's son, whom she had at the age of 16. Maya's son, Guy, became the new meaning in her life.

I thoroughly recommend the coming of age story, *I Know Why the Caged Bird Sings.* It artfully depicts the experience of growing up as an African American in the American South in the 1930s and 1940s. Maya Angelou's talent for putting her soul down onto paper proves that no matter how hard life can get, you can make something of yourself.

1 This passage would most likely be found in

A a fantasy novel

B a magazine article

C an introductory text on creative writing

D an essay about growing up during the Depression

2 The author's purpose in writing this passage was probably to

F recommend a good book

G challenge people to write stories

H explain how to overcome obstacles

J persuade readers to agree with a point of view

3 With which of these statements would the author most likely agree?

A Maya Angelou let the hardships in her life take over.

B Moving around during one's childhood can be traumatic.

C Maya Angelou is a gifted writer and an inspirational woman.

D *I Know Why the Caged Bird Sings* is a dull and boring story.

4 The author of this passage would probably

F help libraries to buy more books

G support research on the Great Depression

H agree that children should live with their parents

J like to read other books written by Maya Angelou

5 Based on the passage, which of these is probably true?

A Maya Angelou's brother didn't like her.

B Maya Angelou's grandmother had a negative influence on her.

C Maya Angelou wanted to get away from her mother's boyfriend.

D Maya Angelou was depressed when her son was born.

6 Which of these techniques does the author use to illustrate the hardships of Maya Angelou's childhood?

F concrete examples

G exaggerated details

H personal testimony

J testimonial from an expert

7 Which of these is an <u>opinion</u>?

A Her first book was about her own experiences.

B Maya's son, Guy, became the new meaning in her life.

C Maya learned many important life lessons from her grandmother whom she lovingly called "Momma."

D It artfully depicts the real experience of growing up as an African American in the American South in the 1930s and 1940s.

Check your answers on pages 93–94.

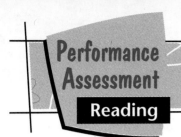

Performance Assessment

Reading

The Reading Performance Assessment is identical to the actual TABE in format and length. It will give you an idea of what the real test is like. Allow yourself 50 minutes to complete this assessment. Check your answers on pages 94–97.

Sample A

When the bright _____ shone directly in our eyes, we couldn't see.

A sun

B color

C shade

D glasses

Sample B

> The sound of breaking glass woke Dave up. The dog started barking. Dave got out of bed, grabbed a baseball bat, and quietly headed downstairs.

Why did Dave get out of bed?

F The dog needed to be fed.

G He felt like playing baseball.

H He needed to fix a broken window.

J He wanted to find out if someone had broken into the house.

Page 68

Go On ▶

TABE Fundamentals: Reading

Read the paragraph about logrolling and the definition of *balance*. The passage says that logrollers "dance atop logs in quick, steady steps while hoping to maintain enough *balance* to outlast their competitors." Use the dictionary entry for the word *balance* to do number 1.

Logrolling began during the early days of logging. Loggers moved fallen logs to the sawmills, using rivers as highways. Log drivers would move the floating logs down river by rolling them with their feet, taking care not to fall and slip underneath the logs. Logrollers today, however, are athletes who dance atop logs in quick, steady steps while hoping to maintain enough balance to outlast their competitors.

bal·ance (bal'əns) *Noun.* 1. A state of equal weight or value. 2. A harmony of design elements. 3. A remainder: *the balance of a checking account.* 4. An instrument for weighing. 5. Bodily or mental stability.

1   Which definition of the word *balance* is used in the passage?

   A Definition 2

   B Definition 3

   C Definition 4

   D Definition 5

Read the passage. Answer numbers 2 through 6 by circling the letter of the best answer.

The men in early American logging camps knew how to take a break from working. They had a contest that kept everyone in great shape. Two men would stand on a long, round log floating in a river. They would roll the log back and forth until one lost his footing and fell off.

Today, people of all backgrounds enjoy this contest. It has become a popular and competitive sport called logrolling. Logrolling may look simple, but winning a logrolling contest requires focus and balance. It only takes one quick step for an experienced roller to send a beginner plunging into the water.

The key is to not look at your feet because this will throw off your rhythm. If you stick your arms out a bit, you can stabilize yourself. Bending your knees and taking quick steps keeps you in motion. You have to remain on your own end of the log at all times, in between the foul lines, which are painted on the log. Touching your opponent is illegal and will cause you to be disqualified.

Knowing how to swim is the only background needed to learn this 100-year-old sport. The next time you are looking to try a safe and exciting new sport, try logrolling. Some people become good at it quickly! It's a great way to improve agility, concentration, and mental toughness.

2 The author's purpose in writing this passage was probably to

   F tell people about a fun and challenging sport

   G entertain people with a logging story

   H explain how logging camps were run

   J persuade people to learn about the history of logrolling

3 Which of these statements is best supported by the passage?

   A Loggers are the best logrollers.

   B Logrolling is a mental and physical workout.

   C People are not interested in logrolling.

   D Becoming a logroller requires many years of training.

4 The passage says that bending your knees will "keep you in *motion*." What does the word *motion* mean here?

   F power

   G energy

   H stillness

   J movement

5 According to the passage, which of the following techniques is not helpful in logrolling?

   A bending your knees

   B taking many quick steps

   C sticking your arms out to your sides

   D focusing your eyes on your feet

6 The way to win a logrolling competition is to

   F roll the most logs into a river

   G be the first one to stand on a floating log

   H be the last one standing on a floating log

   J roll a log to the shore in the quickest time

Study this index page from a book about gardening. Then answer numbers 7 through 11 by circling the letter of the best answer.

TABE Fundamentals: Reading

7 Which of these is listed on Page 30?

   A Trellises

   B Unicorn Plant

   C Laying Turf Grass

   D Controlling Erosion

8 Which of these is another listing for "Supports"?

   F Staking

   G Troughs

   H Planting

   J Tool Sheds

9 Suppose you find several large green worms on your tomato plants and they seem to be eating the tomatoes. On which page will you find information on how to protect your tomatoes from these insects?

   A 91

   B 145

   C 149

   D 244

10 If you want to find out what tools you will need to plant your first vegetable garden, on which page will you look for this information?

   F 135

   G 158

   H 210

   J 211

11 Which of these <u>cannot</u> be found on this index page?

   A Urns

   B Stems

   C Sundials

   D Transplanting

Read the passage about a troublesome insect. Answer numbers 12 through 19 by circling the letter of the best answer.

We have all heard stories of human invasions, both historical and fictional. But, can you believe that an ant is considered to be one of the most damaging invaders that the United States has ever seen? Red imported fire ants are thought to have arrived on the Mississippi or Alabama Gulf Coast in the 1930s, as stowaways on ships from South America. The ants "took over" their new home because there were no natural predators for them to deal with. They thrived on plants, animals, and other insects and multiplied at a rapid rate.

Since their arrival, the ants have infested many of the country's southern states including Florida, Alabama, and Texas. Many people who live in these places have to contend with the ants' invasions. Fire ants are aggressive and can cause serious harm to people, animals, and crops.

Fire ants are small, red insects that build mounds of soft soil. When their nests are disturbed, they get very agitated. They can quickly swarm up a person's leg and start biting. Each ant can bite repeatedly, so it's possible for someone to endure multiple bites from only a few ants. When the person moves in response to a bite, the movement can trigger even more ants to climb up and attack. The venom that they inject causes a burning and itching sensation. Some bites leave white blisters on the skin that can become infected if not kept clean.

The ants are not only a nuisance to people. They also pose a threat to animals. They are omnivores that feed on small animals as well as plants. They are responsible for killing certain wildlife species such as quail, deer, lizards, songbirds, and toads. Fire ants have also been known to cause damage to young fruit trees and crops such as corn, okra, and potatoes.

Despite their bad reputation, fire ants are a blessing in disguise to some people. Because the red ant's diet includes insects, they can quickly rid an area of undesired pests. This is good news for areas riddled by ticks. The ants are also helpful in combating termite populations. In addition, they may actually be helpful to some trees by preying on the insects that feed on the tree parts.

However, red imported fire ants continue to have more enemies than friends. There is great hope that in the future we will be able to control the ravages they inflict. In the meantime, fire ants are being controlled by small-scale efforts. Spraying natural and chemical pesticides around and directly onto ant mounds is very effective.

Page 74

Go On ▶

12   The author of this passage would probably

    F   agree that fire ants are a nuisance

    G   like to see fire ants multiply in numbers

    H   support research on the benefits of fire ants

    J   help to introduce fire ants to the northern states

13   The fire ant probably acquired its name because

    A   it is crimson-colored red

    B   it can only be killed by fire

    C   its venom produces a burning sensation

    D   it thrives in hot, desert-like environments

14   Based on the passage, which of the following is probably true?

    F   Fire ants are a threat to large, domestic animals.

    G   Some insects are not native to the United States.

    H   Large populations of fire ants are easy to control.

    J   Some insects can be trained to be useful to people.

15   Fire ants might be useful to an area that has

    A   bird nests and a pond

    B   cornfields and farmlands

    C   a playground for children

    D   livestock infested with ticks

16   According to the passage, why do people dislike fire ants?

    F   They eat termites.

    G   They have a painful sting.

    H   They are difficult to destroy.

    J   They prey on tree-eating insects.

17   Which of these would probably best prevent a skin infection caused by a fire ant?

    A   rubbing the area vigorously

    B   putting ice cubes around the area

    C   washing the area with soap and water

    D   making a compress using sand and bandages

Numbers 18 and 19 are related to using reference sources. Read each item and circle the letter of the best answer.

18   The quickest way to find the location of the Alabama Gulf Coast would be to look in

    F   an atlas

    G   an almanac

    H   a travel guide

    J   a magazine

19   Which of these books would probably be the best source of information about how to make natural pesticides?

    A   *Exploring Nature*

    B   *Recipes for Organic Gardening*

    C   *Protecting our Rivers and Forests*

    D   *A Field Guide to Beneficial Insects*

CUSTOMER FEEDBACK FORM
HAUL-IT YOURSELF
Rental Trucks

Our goal is to provide a great product and excellent service at a low cost. That is why your feedback is so important to us. Please take a few minutes to rate your rental experience. This information will enable us to improve our product, our service, and our company.

Name _____

Date(s) of Rental _____

Rental type/size _____

Pick-up location _____

Drop-off location _____

Where did you hear about us? _____

❏ **CUSTOMER SERVICE AT PICK-UP** Friendliness, courtesy, and efficiency.

_____ Exceptional   _____ Above average   _____ Average   _____ Below average

Comments: _____

❏ **CUSTOMER SERVICE AT DROP-OFF** Friendliness, courtesy, and efficiency.

_____ Exceptional   _____ Above average   _____ Average   _____ Below average

Comments: _____

❏ **CONDITION OF VEHICLE** Clean and in good working order.

_____ Exceptional   _____ Above average   _____ Average   _____ Below average

Comments: _____

❏ **RATES** Value and cost compared to other rental companies.

_____ Exceptional   _____ Above average   _____ Average   _____ Below average

Comments: _____

❏ **AVAILABILITY** Availability of vehicle requested and availability of dates requested.

_____ Exceptional   _____ Above average   _____ Average   _____ Below average

Comments: _____

❏ Other Comments_____

Thank you for choosing HAUL-IT YOURSELF!

Maria got a new job in a different state. She planned to transport all of her furniture and belongings herself. Maria called around to get quotes on rates for a 24-foot truck rental. The HAUL-IT YOURSELF Rental Truck Company had the lowest price, so Maria reserved a truck for the date she needed.

When Maria went to pick up the truck, she had to wait in a long line because there was only one person working that day. When it was finally her turn, the customer service person, Dave, was very attentive to Maria. He answered all of her questions about the truck, and he even showed her how to shift it into reverse.

Maria's move went smoothly. She felt comfortable on the clean seat. The brakes worked well, and the seat belt on the driver's side was functional. Maria felt very safe driving the truck. She was glad that she decided to make the move on her own.

20 This feedback is used to rate the quality of

F a travel company

G a car rental company

H a truck sales company

J a truck rental company

21 Which of these might be written as a comment under "Condition of Vehicle"?

A The truck was dirty and unsafe.

B The interior of the truck was clean.

C The price of the truck was reasonable.

D The truck's safety features were in need of repair.

22 The passage says that Maria's seat belt was *functional*. What does the word *functional* mean here?

F tight

G broken

H working

J standard

23 Which of these statements by Maria is probably related to Dave's customer service skills?

A He was polite and helpful.

B He was rude and impatient.

C He was careful.

D He lacked knowledge about trucks.

24 In what part of the form would Maria write that the service center was understaffed?

F Availability

G Other Comments

H Condition of Vehicle

J Customer Service at Drop-off

25 Which of these is a comment that Maria would probably write about her experience with the HAUL-IT YOURSELF Rental Truck Company?

A The service is slow and the trucks are too old.

B The service is fast and the trucks are luxurious.

C The trucks are too expensive and the people are incompetent.

D The trucks are a great value and the people are knowledgeable.

Read the passage. It is from *Where the Red Fern Grows*, by Wilson Rawls. The book is about a boy and his two dogs. Answer numbers 26 though 32 by circling the letter of the best answer.

All at once the beating stopped. I heard loud cries from the gang. Turning over on my back, I was just in time to see the marshal plant a number-twelve boot in the seat of the last kid. I knew I was next. I wondered if he'd kick me while I was down.

I lay where I was. He started toward me. I closed my eyes. I felt a hand as big as an anvil clamp on my shoulder. I thought, "He's going to stand me up, and then knock me down."

He raised me to a sitting position. His deep, friendly voice said, "Are you all right, son?"

I opened my eyes. There was a smile of his wide, rugged face. In a choking voice, I said, "Yes sir. I'm all right."

He helped me to my feet. His big hands started brushing the dust from my clothes.

"Those kids are pretty tough, son," he said, "but they're really not bad. They'll grow up someday."

"Marshal," I said, "I wouldn't have fought them, but they pulled my pup's ears."

He looked over to my sack. One pup had worked his way almost out through the hole. The other one's head and two little paws were sticking out. Both of them were whimpering.

A smile spread all over the big marshal's face. "So that's what started the fight," he said.

Walking over, he knelt down and started petting the pups. "They're fine-looking dogs," he said. "Where did you get them?"

I told him I had ordered them from Kentucky.

"What did they cost you?" he asked.

"Forty dollars," I said.

He asked if my father had bought them for me.

"No," I said. "I bought them for myself."

He asked me where I got the money.

"I worked and saved it," I said.

"It takes a long time to save forty dollars," he said.

"Yes," I said. "It took me two years."

"Two years!" he exclaimed.

I saw an outraged look come over the marshal's face. Reaching up, he pushed his hat back. He glanced up and down the street. I heard him mutter, "There's not a one in that bunch with that kind of grit."

Picking up my sack, I said, "Thanks for helping me out. I guess I'd better be heading for home."

TABE Fundamentals: Reading

26 Which of these is the best title for this passage?

F "Dogs for Protection"

G "A Battle with the Law"

H "My Childhood Adventures"

J "Help from an Unlikely Source"

27 Which of these probably happened just before the marshal helped the boy up?

A The boy bought two puppies.

B A gang of kids fought the boy.

C The boy went home with his two new pups.

D The boy and a marshal fought each other.

28 With which of these statements would the marshal most likely agree?

F The boy is too young to be working.

G The boy with the dogs is a troublemaker.

H The kids in the gang will act mature as adults.

J The kids in the gang are all thieves and hoodlums.

29 What does the marshal mean when he says, "There's not a one in that bunch with that kind of grit"?

A None of the kids in the gang like to eat grits for breakfast.

B None of the kids in the gang is as dirty and soiled as the boy with the pups.

C None of the kids in the gang is as strong and athletic as the boy with the pups.

D None of the kids in the gang is determined enough to work for two years to save up money for something.

30 If the boy's sister, upon his return home, complained about how mean marshals are, the boy would most likely respond by

F ignoring her to avoid getting into an argument

G disagreeing and telling her about how the marshal helped him

H strongly supporting her viewpoint and adding to the list of complaints

J agreeing with her and enlisting her help to go and confront the local marshal

31 Which of these sentences from the passage expresses a <u>fact</u>?

A They're fine-looking dogs.

B All at once the beating stopped.

C Those kids are pretty tough, son.

D It takes a long time to save forty dollars.

32 By the end of the passage, how have the boy's feelings about the marshal changed?

F from fearful to relieved

G from carefree to cautious

H from curious to indifferent

J from comforted to alarmed

Read the letters that a girl and her grandfather sent to one another. Answer numbers 33 through 37 by circling the letter of the best answer.

Dear Grandpa,

How are you? I'm doing great. School is good too. We started a new social studies unit this week. It is about immigration. I really like it so far. One of our homework assignments is to interview someone who came to America from another country. I thought of you as soon as my teacher described the project.

Mom has been telling me stories about how you came to Ellis Island on a boat from Italy. Did you know that you were one of twenty-two million passengers who came through the port of New York between 1892 and 1924? That is amazing! I can't wait to find out more about what it was like to leave your homeland and what you thought of America when you first stepped off the boat.

I miss you, Grandpa, and I can't wait to talk to you. I know that your stories are going to be really interesting. I hope that I can share them with the class. I'll talk to you soon.

Love,
Sophia

Dear Sophia,

I am so glad that you are interested in learning more about your heritage. I would be honored to help you with your school project.

I left Italy as a young boy. Your great grandfather, my father, wanted a better life for his family. That is why he brought us to America.

My first memory of America was seeing the Statue of Liberty, the golden door to the land of opportunity. Lady Liberty stood tall and seemed to welcome all of us on the boat with her glowing torch that lit our way. The boat anchored and we got off and entered the building. We made our way up the steep steps and I was melting. It was August and we were wearing our thick coats, which wouldn't fit in our overstuffed bags.

I have much more to tell you, Sofia. When you call, I will continue with the story. I have plenty of memories to share with you. I may be old, but my mind is a sharp as a tack!

P.S. When I come to visit over the holiday, I would be happy to go to your school and talk with your class. Let me know if you like this idea.

Much love,
Grandpa Tony

33 What did Grandpa Tony do when he first got off the boat?

   A He entered the building.

   B He took off his thick coat.

   C He went to his new school.

   D He climbed the steep steps.

34 From reading the letters, you could say that Sophia and her grandfather both

   F want to go to Italy

   G like helping others

   H are interested in family history

   J prefer to travel by boat

35 Why does Grandpa Tony offer to go to Sophia's school?

   A in case she needs a ride home

   B to share his memories with her class

   C because he wants to thank her teacher

   D to talk to her teacher about the homework assignment

36 What was "the golden door" to which Grandpa Tony referred?

   F the door of the boat

   G the Statue of Liberty

   H the door to the building

   J the opportunity for a better life

37 What does the word *interview* mean in Sophia's letter?

   A to meet

   B a news article

   C to congratulate

   D to ask questions

Here is a passage describing an interesting theory about weight loss. Read it and then answer numbers 38 through 43 by circling the letter of the best answer.

Let's imagine a common weight loss scenario. You need to lose weight quickly for a special occasion. Desperate for fast results, you go on the latest "crash" diet that promises to help you lose ten pounds in ten days. Amazingly, when you step on a scale, the display shows that your weight has gone down. But is it body fat that you lost? Probably not. Crash diets are not an effective approach to long-term weight loss. What they mainly do is reduce muscle tissue and the amount of water in your body.

When most people start a diet, they reduce their intake of food and water and become dehydrated. The body stores what water it has in its outer tissues because too little water is being consumed. This water reserve leads to the puffed-up or bloated feeling that we have all felt at one time or another.

While on a diet that urges you to drink lots of water, your weight goes down as the body releases the extra water that has been stored in outer tissues. The bloat disappears now that you are well hydrated, but you have not necessarily lost any fat.

Another way that many crash diets compel your body to lose water weight is by restricting calories. By drastically cutting back on the calories you consume, you lose some of the water that your body has been carrying around. This is especially true of high protein, low-carbohydrate diets. When you first stop eating carbohydrates, your body releases water that's stored with its supply of carbohydrates. Therefore, most of the weight lost is from water, not fat. If you return to your old eating habits, the water will be stored again and the weight will come right back on.

Now let's talk about muscle tissue. Lean muscle is the body's most active tissue. Muscle burns calories around the clock. The more you have of it, the more calories you will burn. In order to burn fat, lean muscle must be preserved and even strengthened, if possible.

However, most diets do the opposite of this. They force the body into destroying muscle. Crash diets trick the body into thinking that it is starving. Therefore, as a defense, the body attacks itself and begins to burn its lean muscle. By going after muscle tissue, the body is able to stay alive longer while burning fewer food calories each day.

How can you be sure that it is body fat you are losing when the numbers on the scale go down? If you have been drinking plenty of water each day, you can assume that you are well hydrated. This means that the weight loss is not water. Let's also assume that you are maintaining or increasing your muscle mass through strength and resistance training. You can be confident that you are not losing muscle. Therefore, the weight that you are losing must be body fat.

38 Which of these would be the best title for this article?

F "Diets That Work"

G "Severe Calorie Restriction"

H "Increasing Your Metabolism"

J "Lose Fat, Not Muscle or Water"

39 According to the author of this passage, how might maintaining strength and resistance training affect a person's weight loss program?

A The body would lose weight that is mostly muscle tissue.

B Weight loss would occur because the body would shed extra water weight.

C Muscle mass would remain stable or increase and help the body to burn more calories faster.

D The water supply in the outer tissues of the body would accumulate and cause a person's body to bloat or puff up.

40 Which of these best explains why a person who starts to drink lots of water loses some weight?

F The stomach is fuller because of the extra water, and this causes a person to eat fewer calories.

G The body thinks that there is a readily available source of water, so it sheds extra water reserves.

H The body puffs up because of the extra water weight, and this bloating does not weigh as much as the body fat that is lost.

J Increasing your water intake drastically reduces your body's carbohydrate supply and causes the body to become less bloated or full of water.

41 The fourth paragraph mentions "*restricting* calories." Which of these has the same meaning as the word *restrict*?

A limit

B impose

C exceed

D broaden

42 Which of these weight loss plans is most likely to help a person lose body fat?

F Eat more carbohydrates and less protein.

G Drink plenty of water and strengthen muscles.

H Eat plenty of protein and cut back on water intake.

J Consume fewer carbohydrates and stop strength training.

43 Which of these statements best summarizes the excerpt?

A Crash diets are the best way to lose weight.

B Increasing your body's muscle tissue will also increase your body's metabolic rate.

C The key to long-term weight loss is to shed the extra water in your body's outer tissues.

D Long-term weight loss involves increasing your body's muscle tissue and keeping your body well hydrated.

This is a passage about a famous twentieth-century American musician. Read the passage. Then answer numbers 44 through 50 by circling the letter of the best answer.

Ray Charles is one of the most successful musicians of all time. He has several gold records and awards, including a cherished Lifetime Grammy Award. His induction into three different musical Halls of Fame attests to the diversity of his talent.

Ray Charles Robinson didn't start out with many advantages. He was born to Aretha and Baily Robinson on September 23, 1930, during the height of the Depression. In his lifetime Ray Charles faced not only poverty and racial prejudice, but he also had to come to terms with the devastating losses of his family and his vision. Amazingly Ray managed to find the strength to believe in himself and his music, despite the enormous obstacles that were thrown his way.

The first major tragedy in Ray's life was the death of his younger brother. When Ray was five years old, his three-year-old brother drowned in a metal washtub full of water. Ray's childhood trauma intensified when he lost his sight. At age six, he was diagnosed with the degenerative eye disease, glaucoma. By age seven, Ray was blind.

The one thing that kept Ray going was his musical studies at St Augustine's School for the Deaf and Blind in Florida. He was admitted to the school on a scholarship. At St. Augustine's, Ray developed his musical gift. He studied classical music, but he felt a passion for jazz and blues. Ray has said that studying classical music was a means to an end. To learn how to arrange and write music, he had to study classical music, but playing jazz and blues was in his heart.

Ray's mother and father passed away, and Ray became an orphan at age 15. He turned to music for comfort and set out on the road to becoming a professional musician. Ray's musical career began to take off after he moved to the west coast. He cut his first professional recording in 1950. The song, "I Got a Woman," became a smash hit.

Ray Charles Robinson shortened his name to Ray Charles, and he traveled around the United States, playing at different clubs. The only damper to his rising success was the racial inequality and segregation with which he had to contend. When he traveled, he had to find gas stations that had restrooms for "colored" people. If he was hungry, he had to find restaurants that would serve blacks.

Once, a show promoter told Ray that he would have to play downstairs to the white audience and the black audience would have to listen from upstairs. Ray cancelled the show and sought moral support in his new friendship with activist, Dr. Martin Luther King, Jr. The commitment to King's cause was in Ray's heart. He helped to raise money through his music to fund the legal expenses of people who were jailed for breaking unfair laws.

Ray Charles went on to have one of the most successful careers in American musical history, recording hit after hit. He achieved worldwide fame and had a profound influence on popular music.

44 This passage would most likely be found in

F a blues magazine

G an introductory text on classical music

H a political newspaper column

J an essay about racial injustice

45 Which of these is probably true of Ray Charles?

A He is best known for his country and western music.

B He could compose music only when he was happy.

C He was influenced by the musical styles of classical performers.

D He became more determined to fight racial injustice as he experienced it in his own life.

46 What did he mean when he said that studying classical music was a means to an end?

F It would give him the training he needed to learn to write and arrange music.

G It allowed him to develop himself as a classical musician.

H He wanted it to end.

J He really wanted to study the blues.

47 According to the passage, Ray Charles acted on a *commitment* to King's cause. In this context, the word *commitment* means the same as

A pledge

B calling

C witness

D yearning

48 Which of these best describes Ray Charles' reaction to the way that he was treated while on tour?

F He was amused by the requests of certain show promoters.

G He was angry because many restaurants didn't have the foods he liked.

H He was overjoyed to have the freedom to travel and stay wherever he wanted.

J He was upset that there were separate facilities for people of different races.

49 According to the passage, what did not happen in Ray Charles' life?

A His father died.

B His mother died.

C His brother died.

D He was hauled into jail.

50 Which of these best summarizes the passage?

F Ray Charles composed and recorded many classical hits during his lifetime.

G Ray Charles showed his respect for Dr. Martin Luther King, Jr., by joining in his protest rallies.

H Ray Charles, a musician, overcame tragic events and shared his gift of music with the world.

J Ray Charles lost his family members and devoted his life to writing about them in his books and recordings.

STOP

Lesson 1 Practice (page 9)

1. A The word *principle* in this paragraph means "a rule of action or conduct." Saving money each month is a "rule of conduct" that the narrator follows. Option B is not correct because the paragraph is not about anything scientific. In option C the word *principle* is not used to describe a person. Option D is not correct because the *principle* is more of "a rule of action" than "a belief"; the *principle* is acted upon and money is saved.

2. G The word *carry* in this paragraph means "to hold onto something and take it somewhere." The pitcher of lemonade was transported or moved. In option F one cannot "continue or extend" a pitcher. In option H, singing is not mentioned in the paragraph. In option J, the paragraph does not mention math equations.

3. D The word *resistance* in this paragraph means "the ability to fight off or overcome." The paragraph is not about fighting for freedom (option A) or about the motion of an object (option B). The paragraph does not describe anything electrical (option C).

Lesson 2 Practice (page 11)

1. B The topic "Siding" and the sub-topic "Patching" are on page 35. Information about repairing a sub-floor is not what is needed (option A). Information about completely removing or taking off vinyl siding is not required for repairing only a small hole (option C). Information about vinyl tiles is not needed (option D).

2. J The topic "Two-slot Receptacle" is *not* listed on this index page. Options F, G, and H are not correct because each of those topics is listed on this index page.

3. C The topic "Suspended Ceilings" is found on page 208. Options A, B, and D are not correct because information on those topics *cannot* be found on page 208. Different page numbers are assigned to those topics.

4. F The page number for bathroom sinks is located under the topic "Sinks" and under the sub-topic "Bathroom" on page 228. Option G is not correct because information on *kitchen* sinks is on page 225. A kitchen sink may require a different type of drain than a bathroom sink. Options H and J are not correct because neither option has to do with sinks.

Lesson 3 Practice (page 13)

1. C A book of quotations would probably have the *most* sayings by a famous president. Options B and D are not correct because these sources don't have many sayings. Option A is not correct because an atlas does not contain sayings.

2. F The *fastest* way would be to look in an atlas for a map of the state of Virginia. Options G and J are not correct because these sources don't usually have state maps in them. Option H is not correct because a magazine probably wouldn't have a state map either.

3. B To give credit to a source, use a footnote. In option A, just highlighting a quotation would not show where it came from. In option C, an author's name does not belong *at the top* of a report. In option D, putting all of the author's books in a bibliography would not show where a particular quote came from.

4. H The book called *Thomas Jefferson's Inventions* would have the *most* information about the inventions of Jefferson. A book about architecture and building designs (option F), a book about writing (option G), or a book about copy machines (option J) would not be useful.

5. B An encyclopedia offers brief, yet comprehensive, articles on a range of subjects and topics. Atlases (option A) and anthologies (option D) do not offer information on people. A book of quotations (option C) would only offer Jefferson's notable quotes.

6. H A local real estate weekly magazine would be a very useful resource. Options F, G, and J do not offer local real estate information.

Lesson 4 Practice (page 17)

1. D This form is used to obtain information about an employee. In this case, Maria is the employee. Options A, B, and C are not correct because obtaining information about a boss, a child, or a spouse is not the purpose of the form.

2. H Maria should not write about her allergy to bee stings in the "Personal Information" section. That belongs in the "Medical Information" section because Maria would need special medicine if a bee stung her. Options F, G, and J are not correct because there are lines to write about each of these in the "Personal Information" section.

3. D There are lines in the "Emergency Contact Information" for the name and phone numbers of the person to contact in case of an emergency. The emergency contact (Maria's husband) would be the first person to be called if something happened to Maria at work. Options A, B, and C are incorrect because those sections do not ask for another person's name and contact information.

4. F If Maria got hurt at work, a doctor would need to see the information on the form. The directions on the form say that the information "will be kept private." It is not likely that employees, children, or parents (options G, H, and J) would be permitted to see the form.

5. A Maria would need special medicine if a bee stung her. Her allergy to bee stings should be written in the "Medical Information" section. Options B and D are not correct because that information belongs in the "Personal Information" section. The form does not ask for any of Maria's certification numbers (option C).

Lesson 5 Practice (page 19)

1. C A book is written or printed material. There are four books altogether. Option A is not correct because that is how many cassettes there are on the display. Option B is not correct because that is how many audio (cassette and record) selections there on the display. Option D is too many.

2. J *Constructing a Modern Church* is a video, so it can be watched. Because "constructing" means "building," the video must be about building a church. Options F and G are not correct because they are not videos. Option H is not correct because it is a video tour of churches that have *already* been built.

3. D The best choice for Madge would be to read the book called *Gothic Churches. Great Churches of the 17th Century* is about all churches during this time, not just Gothic style churches (option A). Although Notre Dame is a gothic cathedral, Madge is interested in reading about many different churches, not just one (option B). Madge is not interested in looking at pictures of stained glass (option C).

4. F The question says that Madge wants to listen to the music selection on her record player. Option F is a record. Options G, H, and J are not correct because they are not records.

Lesson 6 Practice (page 21)

1. C According to the compass rose, Vining Hill is southwest of Hosmer Corner. In options A and D going north from Hosmer Corner would take you further away from Vining Hill. In option B, southeast is the opposite direction.

2. H According to the compass rose, Hosmer Corner is the furthest east. Options F, G, and J are not correct because on the map, they are all further west than Hosmer Corner.

3. A On this map, 168 to 202 to 57 is the correct route. Options B and D will not take you to either location. Option C takes you *from* Hosmer Corner *to* Congamond Lakes.

TABE Review: Interpret Graphic Information (pages 22–23)

1. B *Elvis: The Early Years* is the only title of the results that can be *heard*; it is a cassette. Options A, C, and D are book titles. Books are *read*, not heard. [Library Catalog Display]

2. F The *fastest* way to find the location of a small town would be to look in an atlas for a map of the state of Tennessee. Options G and H are not correct because an almanac and a travel magazine probably wouldn't include a state map of Tennessee. Option J is not correct because poems, not maps, are found in an anthology of poetry. [Reference Sources]

3. B Interstate 40 is a direct route from Jackson southwest to Memphis. Highway 45 (option A) runs north-south. Interstate 55 (option C) does not pass anywhere near Jackson. Highway 79 (option D) runs southwest into Memphis, but it is not the best choice because Interstate 40 is closer to Jackson than Highway 79 is. [Maps]

4. H Page 76 can be found under the heading of *Smith, Junior* and then under the sub-heading of *recording sessions*. In option F, page 29 has information on Junior Smith and *Elvis's army service*. In option G, page 33 has information on recordings with Gordon Stoker. In option J, page 99 has information on TV appearances with Ed Sullivan. [Index]

5. C Amy would have liked to have seen the meditation garden and she could let the tour group know that by writing it down on the "Comments/Feedback" lines. The paragraph says that Amy *did* see the trophy building (option A). Amy Chan is Amy's name, and that information goes on the line that says "Name" (option B). Amy did not see the meditation garden (option D). [Forms]

6. G When she sees Elvis's tombstone, she has to hold back (or restrain) her tears. Options F, H, and J do not fit with the meaning of the sentence. Amy is not "grasping" her tears (option F), "regarding" her tears (option H), or "occupying" her tears (option J). [Dictionary Usage]

Lesson 7 Practice (page 25)

1. C The word *whipping* in this paragraph means "blowing." It makes sense because wind blows. *Whipping* also means "beating" (option A), but that answer does not fit with the meaning of the sentence. *Whipping* can mean "mixing," but that answer does not fit with the meaning of the sentence (option B). Option D is not correct because *whipping* does not mean "singing."

2. J The word *adorned* in this paragraph means "decorated." It makes sense because wings are decorated with feathers. *Adorned* does not mean the same as *adhered, admired,* or *traveled* (options F, G, and H).

3. B The word *scanned* in this paragraph means "searched." It makes sense because searching means the same as *looking,* another word in the sentence. In one context, *scanned* can mean *copied* (option A), but that answer does not fit with the meaning of the sentence. *Scanned* does not mean the same as *swindled* or *traversed* (options C and D).

4. G The word *determined* in this paragraph means "steadfast." It makes sense to say: "The urgency of my search kept me focused and determined *(steadfast)."* *Determined* does not mean the same as *awake, defeated,* or *delighted* (options F, H, and J).

5. D The word *effortlessly* in this paragraph means "without force." It makes sense to say: "floating effortlessly *(without force)* through the cold night air." *Effortlessly* does not mean the same as "without pain" (option A), "without warmth" (option B), or "without warning" (option C).

6. H The word *tingle* in this paragraph means "a prickling sensation." It makes sense to say: "the tingle *(a prickling sensation)* of hunger." *Tingle* does not mean the same as "a cold sensation" (option F), "a sudden movement" (option G), or "a feeling of alertness" (option J).

TABE Review: Words in Context (pages 26–27)

1. B In this sentence the word *aroma* means "scent." The author could smell the scent of the chicken cooking. Options A and D are words that have to do with eating, and the passage doesn't mention eating the chicken until the second paragraph. Option C is not correct because aroma has to do with the sense of smell, not sight.

2. H In this sentence the word *indulge* means "to gratify" or "satisfy." The author was indulging, or gratifying, herself or himself by eating the drumstick. In option F *indulge* in this context does not mean "to eat," although eating is one form of indulgence. In option G "to cover" means "to hide." In option J "to embrace" means "to hold."

3. D In this sentence the word *emerged* means "came out of." It makes sense to say, "The feast came out of the kitchen." Options A, B and C are not correct because they are not definitions of *emerged*.

4. H The word *drag* means "move slowly" in the context of this sentence. *Slow-motion* is a clue. It means slow movement. Although "pull" (option F) and "search" (option G) are correct definitions for the word *drag*, they do not fit with the meaning of the sentence. Option J is not correct because it contradicts the meaning of *slow-motion*.

5. D The word *beneath* means "underneath or below." The meat or fruit of a pomegranate is underneath its skin. It cannot be above (option A), beside (option B), or around (option C) its skin.

6. F In the context of this sentence, the word *sculptor* means "an artist who carves or makes objects of art." Although a builder (option G) can work with wood, a builder doesn't usually *carve* wood. A butcher (option H) works with meat. An engineer (option J) plans or designs large structures.

7. A The word *unsettled* means "uneasy" in the context of this sentence. The author was uneasy, or uncomfortable, with the way his grandmother's stockings looked. Although the stockings may have looked uneven (option B), this word is not a correct definition for *unsettled*. Although "not paid" (option C) is one correct definition, it does not fit with the meaning of the sentence. Option D is not a correct definition and contradicts the meaning of the sentence.

8. G The word *mimicked* means "imitated" or "copied." The children wanted to imitate, or act like, their grandfather. The children in the story were not trying to entertain or amuse (option F) their grandfather. They were not trying to annoy or irritate (option H) him either. Their grandfather wasn't meeting anyone in the story so he didn't need to be introduced (option J).

Lesson 8 Practice (page 29)

1. D The second paragraph states that Spanish explorers brought horses to North America. Option A is not correct because *sky dogs* is what the horses were called. Option B is not correct because although the Native Americans believed that the Great Spirit was responsible for the horses, they were actually brought by the Spanish. In option C, the Native Americans did not bring horses to the Plains. They just owned and used them.

2. F The first paragraph states that "the early Native Americans of the Plains traveled and hunted by foot." Traveling *by foot* means walking. Dogs were used to pull supplies, not for riding (option G). The *early* Native Americans couldn't have used horses (option H) because they didn't have horses before the Spanish brought them. The passage does not mention wagons (option J).

3. C The last paragraph describes how horses "increased the supply of food and improved mobility." Option A is not correct because the passage does not mention how the horses looked. Option B is not correct because horses were believed to be a gift from the Great Spirit, not brought by people. Just because the horses were compared to dogs (option D), that was not enough of a reason to cherish them.

4. G The last paragraph states that "horses could also pull heavier loads than the dogs." Options F, H, and J are incorrect because the passage does not mention that horses were used to train dogs, carry children, or guard teepees.

5. D The second paragraph says that the horses were thought to be large dogs, "sent as a gift from the Great Spirit of the sky." The passage does not mention that the horses chased dogs (option A). In option B, horses are compared to dogs, not birds. Although the horses were believed to be a gift, the passage did not state that they were thought to have fallen from the sky (option C).

Lesson 9 Practice (page 31)

1. C The first thing that Lance did after his recovery from cancer was to get back into shape. According to the passage, Lance got married *after* he began getting back into shape (option A). The birth of Lance's baby happened *last* in the passage (option B). Lance won the Tour de France as a result of, or *after*, getting back into shape (option D).

2. **J** The passage says that Lance got married in 1998. This happened *before* July and October of 1999 (options F and G). Option H is not correct because he won the Tour de France in July of 1999, during the year *after* his marriage.

3. **A** Lance got back into shape *after* his recovery from cancer, not before he got sick with cancer (option B). Option C is not correct because Lance's baby was born *after* the Tour de France. Option D is not correct because Lance got back in shape *before* winning the Tour de France.

4. **G** The *last* event that happened in this passage is that Lance's baby was born. All the other events in the passage (options F, H, and J) happened before Luke's birth.

Lesson 10 Practice (page 33)

1. **D** The companies that make and sell BGH would make the most money. Options A and C are not correct because the federal government would use taxpayers' money to offset the costs related to a surplus of milk. Option B is incorrect because small dairy farms would *not* benefit. In fact, some would be forced out of business.

2. **H** The article says that "BGH has been linked to cancer and other diseases in dairy cows." Options F and G are not correct because the article does not say that BGH makes cows more fertile or aggressive. Option J is incorrect because BGH *increases*, not *decreases*, the milk production of dairy cows.

3. **D** The last paragraph states that "the government will have to buy the additional milk." It goes on to say that this money would come from the taxpayers. The article doesn't say that the surplus in milk will bring prices down (option A). The article doesn't make any statement regarding health benefits to taxpayers (option B). If small dairy farmers go out of business, there may be *fewer* brands of milk on supermarket shelves (option C).

4. **F** The first paragraph says that "Canada has banned the use of BGH." Option G is not correct because if Canada has dairy farms, then Canadian dairy farms *could* have a need for a product that would help increase the supply of milk. Options H and J are not correct because they contradict the information in the paragraph.

TABE Review: Recall Information (pages 34–35)

1. **C** The article suggests changing your routine in order to "shock" the muscles and get past a plateau. Options A and D are not correct because the article doesn't mention running or doing repetitions. Option B contradicts what the article says about increasing the amount of weights you use. [Stated Concepts]

2. **J** The article gives examples of how to change your routine. One example suggests using the leg press once every ten days if you currently use it once every five days. Options F and H are not correct because adding more weight or using more free weights is not mentioned in reference to the leg press. The article doesn't suggest stopping exercise altogether (option G). [Details]

3. **D** The second paragraph says that "it's common to plateau by doing the same thing again and again." A plateau is when you stop seeing results. In option A, using the weight-lifting circuit wouldn't be a reason to plateau. In option B, bodybuilders would *start* seeing results if they tried new workouts. In option C, food isn't mentioned in the article. [Stated Concepts]

4. **G** "Shock training" is described in the article as varying or changing your workout routine. The third paragraph gives the example of replacing bench presses with some flies. Options F and H are not correct because neither food nor friends are mentioned in the article. Option J is not correct because doing the same routine would contradict the main point of the article. [Details]

5. **A** The first paragraph describes how Arnold was upset or unhappy "because his father never praised his best efforts." Option B contradicts this information. In option C, the passage doesn't mention whether or not Arnold's father came to his competitions. Option D is not correct because Arnold's father did not want Arnold to be a bodybuilder, and he most likely didn't want to be one himself. [Stated Concepts]

6. **H** The last paragraph says that Arnold was 20 years old when he won first place in the Mr. Universe Competition. Option F is not correct because in 1966 Arnold won *second* place in the Mr. Universe Competition. Option G is not correct because Arnold was 18 when he joined the army. Option J is not correct because Arnold won the competition *after* he joined the army. [Sequence]

7. **C** The second paragraph says that Arnold broke into the gym to work out. Options A and B are not correct because the passage doesn't say he went home or waited outside. The passage doesn't mention a second gym (option D). [Details]

8. **H** The first sentence says Arnold was born in Austria. Germany, France, and Belgium (options F, G, and J) are not mentioned in the passage. [Details]

Lesson 11 Practice (page 37)

1. **A** In the first paragraph, Linda writes to Carlos that they "used to joke around." The paragraph doesn't mention what kind of food Carlos and Linda like to eat (option B). Carlos already has a job working at the shelter (option C). Option D is incorrect because although Linda may have had trouble sleeping in her car, the letter doesn't mention how Carlos sleeps.

2. H In her letter, Linda mentioned that the scariest time in her life was when she had to sleep in her car. That was probably why she went to stay at the shelter. She had to sell her furniture for money and because she no longer had a place to keep it (option F). Linda could joke around with Carlos when she was living at the shelter, and her life wasn't going smoothly then (option G). Option J is incorrect because the letter doesn't mention Linda's health.

3. D Linda seemed grateful and thankful that The Lodge was there when she was going through a tough time. The letter didn't mention that The Lodge was closing (option A). Linda describes the first person she met at The Lodge as having a friendly smile (option B). Linda writes that when she was able to get an apartment, she was glad "to get back on [her] feet again" (option C).

Lesson 12 Practice (page 39)

1. B The passage is mostly about the life of Jacques Cousteau, a famous inventor and underwater explorer. Options A and D are incorrect because the TV show and the Cousteau Society were mentioned only to highlight accomplishments in Cousteau's life. Option C is incorrect because the passage doesn't tell about *how* the mines were used. It tells about how the aqua-lung was used to detect mines.

2. J The passage is a short summary or description of Jacques Cousteau's life. The passage doesn't give details about the *Calypso* (option F). Cousteau (option G) didn't write the passage. It was written about him. Option H is incorrect because the only famous French explorer mentioned is Cousteau.

3. A Cousteau's life was devoted to the ocean. He educated others on this topic by writing books, making movies, and inventing equipment that show what life is like in the ocean. Options B and D are incorrect because fighting in World War II and having a family are only briefly mentioned in the passage. Option C is incorrect because Cousteau *invented* the aqua-lung. The passage didn't say that he taught people how to use it.

4. H The first sentence of the fourth paragraph answers the question. Option F is not correct because 1910 is the year Cousteau was born. Option G is not correct because 1933 is the year Cousteau joined the French Navy. Option J is not correct because 1997 is the year Cousteau died.

Lesson 13 Practice (page 41)

1. B This summary includes the *subject*: the job of an animal control worker; the *action*: using pet microchips; and the *outcome*: locating pet owners faster. The passage doesn't mention anything about how hard it is to find people to do the job (option A). Options C and D are incorrect because they are facts from the passage; they don't include enough information to be complete summaries.

2. H Option H summarizes how the chips make it easier to reunite lost pets with their owners. Options F, G, and J are details, but are not the main reason why the chips make finding a lost pet's owner easier.

3. D According to the passage, animal control workers have to catch animals, transport them to shelters, and fill out paperwork to help locate pet owners. Option A is incorrect because the workers don't enter information into the database; they access or use it. Options B and C are job descriptions that are not included in the passage.

Lesson 14 Practice (page 43)

1. C The passage states that if someone has a large tumor on the larynx, it could result in the removal of the voice box. A history of smoking (option A) or a small neck lump (option B) is not reason enough to remove the voice box. The passage does not say anything about removing a voice box if a person can not communicate (option D).

2. G The passage refers to a special device that can help a person speak. It does not say that the device is a computer with a mechanical voice (option H). Option F is not true; a person cannot get a new voice box. Laser surgery (option J) is used to treat some kinds of throat cancer, but it is not used to help with speech.

3. A The fourth paragraph includes information to support the statement in option A. Options B, C, and D are not supported by the passage.

4. F It is a good idea to quit smoking because the damage tobacco smoke causes can turn into cancer. Options G, H, and J are all true statements, but they are not the most important reason to quit. Avoiding cancer is the most important reason to quit.

Lesson 15 Practice (page 45)

1. D In the beginning, Jennifer felt homesick for holiday traditions. After Diego told her that they celebrate similar traditions in her new neighborhood, she felt comforted. Options A, B, and C are not supported by the passage.

2. G Jennifer and Diego both talked about memories of the same holiday traditions. Options F, H, and J are not supported by the passage.

3. B The passage is about a woman realizing that you can feel at home wherever you are. Option A is not the main idea of the passage, and it is not true. Options C and D are both true details from the passage, but they do not summarize the entire passage.

4. J Jennifer was homesick because she missed holiday traditions that were special to her. Options F and G are not reasons why she would be homesick. There is nothing in the passage to support the statement in option H.

1. B The salamander crossing is made up of two tunnels that allow salamanders to safely cross the road in order to get to the pond. The crossing is for salamanders to use, not for people to use (options A and D). The crossing is not a warning sign (option C) for the tunnel.

2. H The passage said that the "critters were getting squashed by careless drivers." This means they were getting run over by cars. The passage didn't say that the salamanders found another pond (option F) or that they laid their eggs in puddles (option G). It didn't mention police officers (option J).

3. A The sign shows the location of the tunnels that the salamanders use to migrate to the pond. The last sentence says that the entrance to the tunnels is below the sign. The sign is not to warn drivers to slow down (options B and D). The salamanders are no longer in danger now that they have tunnels. The sign marks the location of the tunnels, not the pond (option C).

4. H The article says that the residents were "relieved" that the salamander crossing was built. Putting slots in the tunnels (option F), parking at the train station (option G), and the distance between the tunnels (option J) are not ways that residents showed "relief."

1. B These facts are both in the passage and they support the statement. Althea rose to the top of the tennis world even though she grew up poor. Option A is incorrect because the passage doesn't say that Althea graduated from high school. The facts in options C and D are in the passage, but they don't support the statement because they are not examples of "rising to the top."

2. H According to this passage, the sport did not immediately recognize Althea based on her skill alone. She won the New York state championship six times before she was allowed into the United States Lawn Tennis Association. The passage does not have information to support options F and J. Option G contradicts information in the passage; when she started playing, Althea did not have access to good coaches.

3. D Option D is the best answer because Althea was banned from most public tennis courts early in the story and she became the top player in the world at the end of the story. Option A is not correct because Althea was not ignored at the end of her career. Options B and C and are not correct because Althea was not celebrated or acknowledged early in her career.

1. C The author describes the story of how his family acquired their family home. "The Story of My Life" (option A) is not correct because the passage is not all about the author's life. Option B is incorrect because it includes just a little information about life as a migrant worker. The passage does not describe how to grow fruits and vegetables (option D). [Main Idea]

2. G Habitat for Humanity helped the author's family build a house that they otherwise would not have been able to afford. Habitat for Humanity builds permanent homes for families, not temporary homes for migrant workers (option F). Option H is not the best answer because Habitat for Humanity serves and helps families; the volunteers just provide the work. Option J is incorrect because Habitat for Humanity is about housing, not farming. [Conclusion]

3. D The author's father said he wanted "a better life for his family." The author's father didn't lose his job (option A); he quit it. He got a job in a grocery store (option B) after he made the decision to settle down. The statement in option C is not supported by the passage. [Cause and Effect]

4. F The mother wanted to "raise a family and teach them the value of education." This means that she wanted her own children to go to school. She wanted her own house, not her own farm (option G). The author's mother did not want to move back into her parent's house (option H). Option J is incorrect because she paid for her own college tuition. [Conclusion]

5. C The last two paragraphs are about how the organization Habitat for Humanity improved the living situation of the author's family. Option A is not the best answer because the passage is the story of one family, not one town. Option B is incorrect because the author's father did not go to college. The man and the woman in the passage do not live in Mexico (option D). [Summary and Paraphrase]

6. G Before the author's father had a family of his own, he seemed content with living as a migrant worker. When his family started to grow, he became dissatisfied with his job; he wanted a better life. The father was not bored (option F), disenchanted (option J), or resentful (option H) anywhere in the passage. [Compare and Contrast]

7. D The first paragraph states that for the author's father home was wherever the next harvest was. Option A is incorrect because the house was simple, not expensive. If option B were true, then the family wouldn't have needed Habitat for Humanity's help. The passage contradicts option C. The author's mother grew up in a crowded house with only one bed. [Supporting Evidence]

8. H The father's old and new jobs both have to do with produce, but the new job does not require him to move from farm to farm. Option F is incorrect because both jobs involve working with food. Option G is incorrect because working in a grocery store doesn't involve traveling. Option J does not reflect the meaning of the quote. [Conclusion]

9. A Option A is correct because he considered his family's welfare first and decided to settle down after he got married. The passage does not say that he prefers traveling (option B). Option C is not supported by the passage. The passage does not mention whether he enjoys building houses. [Character Aspects]

10. G The passage supports this statement. Option F is not true; the family does know its history. Option H is not correct because it is not true. Option J is not correct because the house is "simple but sturdy," not fancy. [Character Aspects]

Lesson 18 Practice (page 53)

1. A The word *spectacular* indicates an opinion or a personal view of the author. Options B, C, and D are all facts that are stated in the letter.

2. J According to the letter, the park was, in fact, donated by Percival P. Baxter. Options F and G are opinions. Option H is neither a fact nor an opinion. It is a request from the author to the readers of the letter.

3. C Not everyone may feel that logging would ruin the park's beauty. According to the letter, Baxter State Park is located in Maine (option A). Ponds are sometimes used for fishing and canoeing (option B). According to the letter, people do hike and camp in Baxter (option D).

4. J Option J is a fact because all these animals do live in the park. Options F, G, and H all include the word *should*, which is used to express an opinion.

Lesson 19 Practice (page 55)

1. B The tour guide is a big supporter of hydro-dams as an inexpensive and clean form of energy. He would probably like to see more of them around the world. Windmills (option A) are not mentioned in the passage. Hydro-dams use river water, therefore the tour guide wouldn't think it should only be used for drinking (option C). The tour guide talks about the benefits of dams and would therefore not agree with option D.

2. H She would probably tell them what she learned as a way of getting them more interested. Trisha probably wouldn't talk about her career plans until she could explain why she thought hydro-dams were important (option F). Trisha was impressed, so she probably wouldn't ignore them (option G). By the end of the story, Trisha didn't have any complaints (option J).

3. A The tour guide has a lot of information and knowledge about how hydro-dams convert water to energy. Other types of power plants are not mentioned (option B). The tour guide doesn't say how much electricity is enough (option C). The tour guide doesn't express an opinion about what consumers should or shouldn't do (option D).

4. H Trisha marveled at the machinery in the dam. Option F is not correct because Trisha said she would like to work on turbines, and turbines are part of dams. Option G is not correct because the tour guide mentioned refrigerators, not Trisha. Option J is not correct because Trisha thought about her new computer game twice during the passage.

Lesson 20 Practice (page 57)

1. C The passage states that the invention of the steamboat led to new trading posts, which in turn led to more trading with remote villages. This caused isolated tribes to have increased exposure to the infected goods that were being traded for buffalo hides. The steamboat would make travel easier, not more difficult (option A). Option B is not correct because trading does not usually involve money. The steamboat would not be a source of anger or confrontation among traders (option D); it helped their businesses grow.

2. G The passage says that smallpox was brought to North America from Europe. Option F is not correct because the passage states that Europeans were often protected from catching the disease because they had been exposed to it. Exposure had helped them develop a resistance to it. The Native American population did not grow and expand, and the culture did not either (option H). Smallpox was brought across the Atlantic Ocean. (option J).

3. A The best answer is A because all people, including Native Americans, can now be protected against some diseases by getting vaccinations. Blankets aren't the main cause of the spread of diseases today (option B). Face masks might protect people from some diseases (option C), but it is not the best answer because not all diseases are airborne. Because diseases can be brought to America, staying in America (option D) would not prevent someone from coming into contact with a disease.

Lesson 21 Practice (page 59)

1. D The reason that the author wrote the article is to describe some steps that are useful in finding and getting a job. The author is not telling a story about someone (option A). The part about preparing a resume does not say how to write a resume (option B). The article is written for job seekers, not employers (option C).

2. G The author thinks that readers will be happy with a job that pays well and interests them. The author doesn't try to persuade readers to agree with a particular point of view (option F). The article is intended to help people find a paying position, not a volunteer one (option H). The article doesn't explain how to find the classified section (option J).

3. A Option A is the best answer because it succinctly describes the entire article. Options B and D address only details, while option C is not correct because the article is not about benefits.

4. G The introductory paragraph supports the statement in option G. The entire article is about how preparation will bring results. Options F and H are true, but they are small details, not the big picture. Option J is not correct because it is vague.

1. **A** In Letter A, the writer says fees should be charged for use of the school bus, just like fees are charged for the use of public transit. Because the author believes in a fee for school bus use, he or she probably wouldn't support people who refused to pay that fee (option B). The author probably wouldn't want to help to pay for other people's children to ride the bus (option C). Option D is incorrect because the author states that only families who use the service should have to pay for it.

2. **H** In letter B, the author wants school bus service to remain free. This means that cities and towns would continue to cover the costs. The author does not want to pay for a bus fee, so he or she would not want to pay for tuition, which would be far more expensive than school bus fees (option F). The author thinks that every child should be able to have a free bus ride to school, so there would be no need for carpools (option G). The author wouldn't support a tax increase (option J) because he or she thinks that enough taxes are already paid.

3. **C** The author is expressing an opinion in the letter. Options A, B, and D are not correct because the author's main purpose was not to give information, report news, or tell a story; It was to express an opinion.

4. **F** Option F is correct because many families do depend on school buses. Options G, H, and J communicate opinions with the words *should*, *it's not right*, and *are meant*.

1. **C** The author calls the umbilical cord's blood a "lifeline," or life-saving treatment for people who have leukemia. The passage does not mention accident victims (option A). The passage doesn't describe how blood is given to hospital patients (option B) or how umbilical cords are removed from newborn babies (option D).

2. **F** The author of this passage uses personal testimonial by telling of his or her own experience as a leukemia survivor. The passage does not give a testimonial from an expert (option J) and it does not exaggerate any details (option G). Option H is incorrect because the author does not use any examples.

3. **C** The last sentence of the passage explains that 10,000 babies are born every day. Each baby is a "possibility of hope." The passage does not support the statements in options A, B, and D.

4. **F** Umbilical-cord blood can possibly cure many life-threatening diseases, which is a second chance at life. The passage mentions medical treatments, but does not discuss medicine (option G). It does not address harvesting bone marrow (option H) or ways of giving birth (option J).

1. **D** The passage is about the basics of soil. This passage is not about how to cook (option A). It is factual, so it can't be science fiction (option B). It does not report on news or a current event (option C).

2. **G** This information would likely be found in a book or magazine about gardening. This topic would probably not be found in the newspaper (option F). A textbook on insects would be mostly about insects, not growing vegetables (option H). The topic of improving soil is informational or non-fiction. It wouldn't be found in a fictional novel (option J).

3. **A** The passage offers information about soil. It does not report news (option B), entertain (option C), or tell a story (option D).

4. **G** The phrase *need to* in option G expresses an opinion. The author thinks people need to look after and care for soil, but not everyone would agree with this. Options F, H, and J are facts.

1. **B** This passage could be found in a magazine that includes book reviews. The passage is about a novel; it is not actually one (option A). Option C is incorrect because the passage doesn't explain how to write; it describes the childhood of a particular writer. The passage is not about the Great Depression; it's about a book that was set during that time period (option D). [Genre]

2. **F** The author of this review recommends a book to readers. The article does not try to motivate readers to write stories (option G). It doesn't tell how readers can overcome obstacles; it tells us that one woman overcame them (option H). Option J is incorrect because the author only tries to interest, not persuade, readers. [Author's Purpose]

3. **C** The author enthusiastically describes Angelou's life story. Option A contradicts the review, which tells how Maya Angelou does overcome hardships. The author doesn't express an opinion about moving around during childhood (option B). Option D contradicts the positive statements in the review. [Apply Passage Elements]

4. **J** The author "thoroughly recommends" the book and would probably be interested in reading more books by the same author. The author doesn't mention an interest in supplying books to libraries (option F). The author is more interested in reading about the "experience of growing up as an African American in the American South in the 1930s and 1940s," not in the general topic of the Great Depression (option G). The author does not express an opinion about whether or not children should live with their parents (option H). [Point of View]

5. **C** The passage says that Maya Angelou was abused by her mother's boyfriend, so she probably wanted to get as far away from him as possible so he couldn't keep hurting her. Option A is incorrect because

Maya must have liked her brother; she changed her name to the nickname he gave her. Option B contradicts the passage; Maya's grandmother "taught her to have pride in herself." Option D contradicts the passage; Maya's son "became the new meaning in her life." [Generalizations]

6. **F** The author illustrates the hardships of Maya Angelou's childhood by giving examples of difficult times in her life, such as leaving home and being abused. The author does not exaggerate the hardships, but just honestly describes them (option G). The author was not a part of Maya Angelou's life so he or she couldn't give a personal testimony about it (option H). There are no experts mentioned in the passage (option J). [Style Techniques]

7. **D** The words "artfully depicts" express the opinion that the author thinks the book is well-written. Options A and B are facts; Maya was happy that she had a baby. It is also a fact that Maya learned lessons about life from her grandmother (option C). [Fact and Opinion]

Performance Assessment: Reading (pages 68–85)

A. **A** Staring into the sun can make it hard to see. Looking at color (option B) and shade (option C) do not affect one's vision. Glasses don't *shine* in people's eyes (option D); they are worn on people's eyes.

B. **J** Dave went to see if there was an intruder in the house. Option F is incorrect because most likely the dog was barking because of the noise. Dave took a baseball bat for protection, not with which to play baseball (option G). He did not know for sure if a window was broken (option H).

1. **D** The word *balance* in this sentence means "bodily or mental stability." One must stay physically balanced, or stable, on a log to remain on top of it while it is rolling. Option A is incorrect because the passage is not about design. Option B is incorrect because a *remainder* is used to refer to math or money. Option C is incorrect because the passage does not mention using an instrument in the sport of logrolling. [Dictionary Usage]

2. **F** The author explained what logrolling is and why it is a good sport to consider trying. The passage did not tell a logging story (option G). It did not go into detail about how logging camps were run (option H). Option J is incorrect because the author was not trying to convince readers to learn more about how the sport developed. [Author's Purpose]

3. **B** Option B is correct because the passage discusses the physical aspects and mental benefits of logrolling. Option A is not correct because the passage says that people of all backgrounds enjoy logrolling. Option C is not correct because people are interested in logrolling. Option D is not correct because the passage says that some people pick up the sport quickly. [Supporting Evidence]

4. **J** By bending their knees and taking quick steps, logrollers can keep their movement going in order to stay on the log. Bending one's knees will not give a logroller more *power* (option F) or *energy* (option G). Option H is incorrect because *stillness* means motionless or the opposite of *motion*. [Same Meaning]

5. **D** The passage says that it is not a good idea to look at your feet while attempting logrolling. Options A, B, and C are all recommended in the passage. [Details]

6. **H** The winner is the last one standing on the log. The loser is the first one who falls off the log and into the water. Options F and J are incorrect because the goal is to stay on a rolling log, not to roll logs into a river or onto the shore. The goal is to stay on the log the longest, not to be the first one to stand up (option G). [Conclusion]

7. **C** To the left of page 30 is the listing for "laying turf grass." Information about trellises (option A) is found on page 320; information on the unicorn plant (option B) is found on page 350; information about controlling erosion (option D) is found on page 304.[Index]

8. **F** *See Staking* is listed under the *Supports* heading. Options G, H, and J are incorrect because *Containers*, *Planting*, and *Tool Sheds* are not listed under *Supports*. [Index]

9. **C** Under the topic *Tomatoes*, there is a page number (149) for information about pest and disease control. An insect that eats tomatoes is called a pest. Information about trapping small animals is listed on page 91 (option A). Information about feeding tomatoes is listed on page 145 (option B). Information on toads is listed on page 244 (option D). [Index]

10. **J** A basic list of tools is found on page 211. Information about growing vegetables in troughs is found on page 135 (option F). Information about planting trees is found on page 158 (option G). Information on tool sheds is found on page 210 (option H). [Index]

11. **B** The topic "Stems" is not listed on this index page because it comes before *sun* in the alphabet. Options A, C, and D are all listed on this index page. [Index]

12. **F** The author's point of view is that fire ants are a nuisance. Options G and J are incorrect because they promote the spread of more fire ants, something that the author does not favor. The author probably would not support research on the benefits of fire ants (option H) because he or she reports that they "cause serious harm to people, animals, and crops." [Point of View]

13. **C** The ants are best known for the fire-like burning sensation that the venom in their bite causes. Option A is not the best answer because the passage did not go into detail about the color shade of the ants. Options B and D are not facts, and are not supported by the passage. [Conclusion]

14. G The passage states that the ants originally came from South America. Therefore, they are not native to the United States. Fire ants are probably not much of a threat to large domestic animals because they don't feed on them (option F). Option H is incorrect because the last paragraph states that small areas of fire ants can be controlled and that there is "hope" for future control of large areas. Option J is incorrect because the passage does not mention that the ants can be trained. [Generalizations]

15. D Fire ants eat ticks, so they could be useful in getting rid of a tick population infesting livestock. Fire ants attack birds (option A) and eat crops such as corn (option B). Option C is incorrect because the sting of the fire ant hurts humans. [Conclusion]

16. G The passage goes into detail about the aggressive behavior of the fire ants and the pain that their sting creates. Options F and J are incorrect because these are reasons for people to like fire ants. Option H is not the best answer because it is not the main reason that fire ants are a nuisance. [Stated Concepts]

17. C The white blisters that the sting creates can become "infected if not kept clean." Washing the affected area would keep it clean. Rubbing the area (option A) and putting sand on it (option D) might cause further irritation or even infection. Putting ice cubes around the area (option B) would not help to keep it clean. [Conclusion]

18. F The fastest way to find out where the Alabama Gulf Coast is would be to look in an atlas for a map of the state of Alabama. Options G and J are incorrect because these sources don't usually have state maps in them. Option H is not correct because a general travel guide probably wouldn't have a state map of Alabama either. [Reference Sources]

19. B A book called *Recipes for Organic Gardening* would probably have a recipe or instructions on how to make a natural or organic pesticide for gardens. Option A is incorrect because it probably has general information about natural areas. Option C is incorrect because fire ants are not a threat to rivers. A book about beneficial insects (option D) would not describe ways to wipe out or destroy pests such as fire ants. [Reference Sources]

20. J This form is for customers to give feedback to a truck rental company. Option F is incorrect because Maria did not need the services of a travel company; she moved herself. Option G is incorrect because she rented a truck, not a car. Option H is incorrect because Maria rented a truck; she did not buy one. [Forms]

21. B Maria said that the interior of the truck was clean. Options A and D contradict the information in the passage. Option C is true, but it belongs under the heading *Rates*. [Forms]

22. H The word *functional* means "working." Maria's seat belt worked, so she felt safe driving the truck. Option F is incorrect because *tight* means "constricting" and

Maria said she was comfortable. If the seat belt was *broken,* (option G) Maria would not have felt safe. Option J is incorrect because the word *standard* means "typical or ordinary." [Same Meaning]

23. A Dave helped Maria by answering all of her questions and by showing her how to put the truck in reverse. He was not rude (option B) because he was very attentive to Maria. Option C is incorrect because the passage did not describe Dave as careful; it stated that the center was understaffed. Option D is incorrect because Dave showed that he does know about trucks. [Forms]

24. G This information does not fit under any specific heading descriptions, so it should be written in the *Other Comments* section. The fact that the center was understaffed does not have to do with the *availability* of trucks and rental dates (option F). It also has nothing to do with the *condition* of the vehicles (option H). Maria waited in line at the pick-up location, not the drop-off location (option J). [Forms]

25. D Maria mentioned that the company's price was the lowest and she described how Dave was informative and helpful. Option A and C are incorrect because overall, Maria had a positive experience with the company. Option B is incorrect because the service was slow; Maria had to wait in a long line. [Summary and Paraphrase]

26. J The passage is mostly about a boy who gets help from a marshal from whom the boy didn't expect to get help. Option F is incorrect because it is the boy who is protective, not the dogs. Option G is incorrect because the boy does not fight with the marshal. Rather the marshal befriends him. Option H is not the best answer because the passage only describes one adventure that the boy has. [Main Idea]

27. B The marshal broke up a fight between the boy and the gang of kids. Then he helped the boy get up. The boy probably bought the puppies long before the fight, not just before it (option A). The boy went home with his two new pups after the marshal helped him up (option C). Option D is incorrect because the marshal did not fight with the boy. He helped him. [Conclusion]

28. H The marshal probably thinks the kids in the gang will be more mature as adults because he tells the boy that "they'll grow up someday." Options F and G are incorrect because the marshal respects the boy for working and saving money. Option J is incorrect because the marshal says that the kids are "really not bad." [Apply Passage Elements]

29. D The marshal says this after the boy tells him how long he worked to save money to buy the dogs. The marshal is impressed and thinks that the boy has more "grit," or toughness, than the kids in the gang. There is no mention of breakfast in the passage (option A). The marshal did not comment on the boy's appearance (option B) or athleticism (option C). [Conclusion]

---

30. G The boy would probably disagree with his sister's opinion that marshals are mean because a very nice marshal helped him out. The boy felt strongly about the marshal's kindness, so he probably wouldn't ignore his sister's complaints (option F). Options H and J are incorrect because the boy had a positive opinion of marshals. [Apply Passage Elements]

31. B It is a fact that the beating stopped. The fight was over when the marshal helped the boy get up. Options A, C, and D are opinions held by the marshal. [Fact and Opinion]

32. F In the beginning of the passage, the boy was afraid that the marshal would kick him. At the end, he is relieved that the marshal helped him out. Options G and J are incorrect because the boy's feelings about marshals were negative in the beginning of the passage. Option H is incorrect because the boy did not seem indifferent toward the marshal. He had a pleasant conversation with the marshal and even thanked him. [Compare and Contrast]

33. A The very first thing that Grandpa Tony did when he got off the boat was enter the building. He didn't mention taking off his coat (option B) and he didn't mention going to a new school (option C). Option D is incorrect because he climbed the steps after entering the building. [Details]

34. H Sophia learned some family history from her mom. Her grandfather's memories are part of the family history. Options F and J are incorrect because Sophia and her grandfather don't mention their travel preferences. Grandpa Tony helps Sophia with her project, but the letters don't mention that Sophia helps others (option G). [Character Aspects]

35. B Grandpa Tony offered to go to Sophia's school to talk with her class. Options A, C, and D are incorrect because Grandpa Tony doesn't give these as reasons to visit Sophia's school. [Stated Concepts]

36. J The "golden door" that Grandpa Tony referred to is the opportunity for a better life and future in his new country. Options F and H are incorrect because the "golden door" is not a real door. Option G is not correct because the golden door is not the statue itself, but what the statue symbolizes—the opportunity for a better life. [Style Techniques]

37. D Sophia wants to *interview* her grandfather or "ask questions" about his experience immigrating to the United States. She doesn't have to meet him to interview him (option A). An interview can be part of a news article, but *a news article* is a noun (option B); the word is used as a verb. Option C is not a correct definition of the word interview; *to congratulate* means to "express pleasure at another's good fortune."[Same Meaning]

38. J The article is mostly about how to lose body fat instead of water or muscle weight. Options F and G are incorrect because the article doesn't go into detail about food intake. Option H is an accurate fact from the article, but the entire passage is not about increasing one's metabolism. [Main Idea]

39. C The author states that lean muscle burns the most calories. By maintaining a muscle-building program, the body holds onto its lean muscle mass. Option A is incorrect because it contradicts information in the passage. Options B and D are incorrect because the author does not link strength training to the body's water supply. [Stated Concepts]

40. G According to the passage, when the body is well hydrated, or has plenty of water, it sheds extra water stored in the outer tissues. The author doesn't mention how water intake affects a person's appetite (option F). Options H and J are incorrect because they contradict information in the passage. [Cause and Effect]

41. A The word *restricting* in this passage means "limiting." It is used to describe diets that restrict or limit the number of calories consumed. Option B is incorrect because "impose" means to require or demand. Options C and D are incorrect because they mean the opposite of *restrict*. [Same Meaning]

42. G The last paragraph states that you can only be sure that your weight loss is body fat through strength and resistance training and by staying well hydrated. Options F, H, and J are incorrect because they contradict the advice that the author gives on how to lose body fat. [Apply Passage Elements]

43. D The author advises readers to lose fat and states that staying hydrated and increasing one's lean muscle through strength training helps to achieve this. Option A contradicts the passage. Options B and C are incorrect because they are single statements from the passage; they are not a complete summary. [Summary and Paraphrase]

44. F The blues is one style of music for which Ray Charles is famous. The article could be found in a magazine of that genre. An introductory book on classical music (option G) would not have a biography of Ray Charles' life because he does not play that style of music. Option H is incorrect because the main theme of the passage is not political. Option J is incorrect because it is more of a biography about a particular person than a paper about general racial injustice. [Genre]

45. D Ray Charles refused to do a segregated show because he was opposed to the racial injustice he experienced while on tour. Ray Charles is best known for recording many styles of music, not just country and western music (option A). Options B and C are incorrect because they contradict information in the passage. [Character Aspects]

46. F The sixth paragraph explains that studying classical music gave Ray Charles the opportunity to learn how to write and arrange music. Option G is not correct because he wasn't particularly interested in becoming a classical musician. Option J is not correct because he did not want it to end. He wanted to take the opportunity to learn so that he could move on to writing and arranging blues and jazz. Option J is not correct because he got something out of studying classical music that he could apply to the music in which he was more interested. [Conclusion]

47. A Ray acted on a *pledge* or a promise to King's cause. Options B and D are incorrect because they do not mean the same as *commitment*. *Calling* and *yearning* are feelings of longing to do something. Option C is incorrect because *witness* means to "observe or testify." [Same Meaning]

48. J The passage described the racial inequality and segregation that Ray experienced at restaurants and gas stations. Ray was not amused or overjoyed by the treatment (options F and H). Ray was angry, but not because of the food (option G). [Stated Concepts]

49. D The passage did not state that Ray ever went to jail. It stated that he raised money for people who went to jail because of unfair laws. Options A, B, and C are incorrect because each of these family members died during Ray's life. [Details]

50. H The passage is about Ray's personal struggles and his triumph through music. The other options are incorrect because they are not true. Ray did not record classical music (option F). The passage did not mention that he joined protest rallies (option G). Ray Charles did not write books about his family (option J). [Summary and Paraphrase]

TABE Review: Interpret Graphic Information
(pages 22–23)

1 Ⓐ Ⓑ Ⓒ Ⓓ
2 Ⓕ Ⓖ Ⓗ Ⓙ
3 Ⓐ Ⓑ Ⓒ Ⓓ
4 Ⓕ Ⓖ Ⓗ Ⓙ
5 Ⓐ Ⓑ Ⓒ Ⓓ
6 Ⓕ Ⓖ Ⓗ Ⓙ
Stop

TABE Review: Words in Context *(pages 26–27)*

1 Ⓐ Ⓑ Ⓒ Ⓓ
2 Ⓕ Ⓖ Ⓗ Ⓙ
3 Ⓐ Ⓑ Ⓒ Ⓓ
4 Ⓕ Ⓖ Ⓗ Ⓙ
5 Ⓐ Ⓑ Ⓒ Ⓓ
6 Ⓕ Ⓖ Ⓗ Ⓙ
7 Ⓐ Ⓑ Ⓒ Ⓓ
8 Ⓕ Ⓖ Ⓗ Ⓙ
Stop

TABE Review: Recall Information
(pages 34–35)

1 Ⓐ Ⓑ Ⓒ Ⓓ
2 Ⓕ Ⓖ Ⓗ Ⓙ
3 Ⓐ Ⓑ Ⓒ Ⓓ
4 Ⓕ Ⓖ Ⓗ Ⓙ
5 Ⓐ Ⓑ Ⓒ Ⓓ
6 Ⓕ Ⓖ Ⓗ Ⓙ
7 Ⓐ Ⓑ Ⓒ Ⓓ
8 Ⓕ Ⓖ Ⓗ Ⓙ
Stop

TABE Review: Construct Meaning
(pages 50–51)

1 Ⓐ Ⓑ Ⓒ Ⓓ
2 Ⓕ Ⓖ Ⓗ Ⓙ
3 Ⓐ Ⓑ Ⓒ Ⓓ
4 Ⓕ Ⓖ Ⓗ Ⓙ
5 Ⓐ Ⓑ Ⓒ Ⓓ
6 Ⓕ Ⓖ Ⓗ Ⓙ
7 Ⓐ Ⓑ Ⓒ Ⓓ
8 Ⓕ Ⓖ Ⓗ Ⓙ
9 Ⓐ Ⓑ Ⓒ Ⓓ
10 Ⓕ Ⓖ Ⓗ Ⓙ
Stop

TABE Review: Evaluate and Extend Meaning
(pages 66–67)

1 Ⓐ Ⓑ Ⓒ Ⓓ
2 Ⓕ Ⓖ Ⓗ Ⓙ
3 Ⓐ Ⓑ Ⓒ Ⓓ
4 Ⓕ Ⓖ Ⓗ Ⓙ
5 Ⓐ Ⓑ Ⓒ Ⓓ
6 Ⓕ Ⓖ Ⓗ Ⓙ
7 Ⓐ Ⓑ Ⓒ Ⓓ
Stop

Performance Assessment: Reading
(pages 68–85)

A Ⓐ Ⓑ Ⓒ Ⓓ
B Ⓕ Ⓖ Ⓗ Ⓙ
1 Ⓐ Ⓑ Ⓒ Ⓓ
2 Ⓕ Ⓖ Ⓗ Ⓙ
3 Ⓐ Ⓑ Ⓒ Ⓓ
4 Ⓕ Ⓖ Ⓗ Ⓙ
5 Ⓐ Ⓑ Ⓒ Ⓓ
6 Ⓕ Ⓖ Ⓗ Ⓙ
7 Ⓐ Ⓑ Ⓒ Ⓓ
8 Ⓕ Ⓖ Ⓗ Ⓙ
9 Ⓐ Ⓑ Ⓒ Ⓓ
10 Ⓕ Ⓖ Ⓗ Ⓙ
11 Ⓐ Ⓑ Ⓒ Ⓓ
12 Ⓕ Ⓖ Ⓗ Ⓙ
13 Ⓐ Ⓑ Ⓒ Ⓓ
14 Ⓕ Ⓖ Ⓗ Ⓙ
15 Ⓐ Ⓑ Ⓒ Ⓓ
16 Ⓕ Ⓖ Ⓗ Ⓙ
17 Ⓐ Ⓑ Ⓒ Ⓓ
18 Ⓕ Ⓖ Ⓗ Ⓙ
19 Ⓐ Ⓑ Ⓒ Ⓓ
20 Ⓕ Ⓖ Ⓗ Ⓙ
21 Ⓐ Ⓑ Ⓒ Ⓓ
22 Ⓕ Ⓖ Ⓗ Ⓙ
23 Ⓐ Ⓑ Ⓒ Ⓓ
24 Ⓕ Ⓖ Ⓗ Ⓙ
25 Ⓐ Ⓑ Ⓒ Ⓓ
26 Ⓕ Ⓖ Ⓗ Ⓙ
27 Ⓐ Ⓑ Ⓒ Ⓓ
28 Ⓕ Ⓖ Ⓗ Ⓙ
29 Ⓐ Ⓑ Ⓒ Ⓓ
30 Ⓕ Ⓖ Ⓗ Ⓙ
31 Ⓐ Ⓑ Ⓒ Ⓓ
32 Ⓕ Ⓖ Ⓗ Ⓙ
33 Ⓐ Ⓑ Ⓒ Ⓓ
34 Ⓕ Ⓖ Ⓗ Ⓙ
Go On

35 Ⓐ Ⓑ Ⓒ Ⓓ
36 Ⓕ Ⓖ Ⓗ Ⓙ
37 Ⓐ Ⓑ Ⓒ Ⓓ
38 Ⓕ Ⓖ Ⓗ Ⓙ
39 Ⓐ Ⓑ Ⓒ Ⓓ
40 Ⓕ Ⓖ Ⓗ Ⓙ
41 Ⓐ Ⓑ Ⓒ Ⓓ
42 Ⓕ Ⓖ Ⓗ Ⓙ
43 Ⓐ Ⓑ Ⓒ Ⓓ
44 Ⓕ Ⓖ Ⓗ Ⓙ
45 Ⓐ Ⓑ Ⓒ Ⓓ
46 Ⓕ Ⓖ Ⓗ Ⓙ
47 Ⓐ Ⓑ Ⓒ Ⓓ
48 Ⓕ Ⓖ Ⓗ Ⓙ
49 Ⓐ Ⓑ Ⓒ Ⓓ
50 Ⓕ Ⓖ Ⓗ Ⓙ
Stop